JOSEPH FIELDING SMITH
A Prophet
Among the People

JOSEPH FIELDING SMITH

A Prophet
Among the People

J M. Heslop and Dell R. Van Orden

Published by
DESERET BOOK COMPANY
Salt Lake City, Utah
1971

Library of Congress No. 77-175121

ISBN No. 87747-454-0

Copyright 1971
by
DESERET BOOK COMPANY

Lithographed by

DESERET NEWS PRESS

in the United States of America

FOREWORD

President Joseph Fielding Smith assumed the presidency of The Church of Jesus Christ of Latter-day Saints exceptionally well qualified by study, experience, and training. He had served for 60 years as an apostle under four Presidents of the Church, 19 years as President of the Quorum of Twelve and five years as a counselor in the First Presidency.

As the son and the grandson of noble men who played important roles in the history of the Church, President Smith literally bridges the gap between the present and the very genesis of the Church. His father, Joseph F. Smith, sixth President of the Church, was born in 1838 in Far West, Missouri, only eight years after the organization of the Church. His grandfather, Hyrum Smith, and his great-uncle, the Prophet Joseph, were martyred in the Carthage Jail, June 27, 1844. President Smith has proven worthy of this great heritage in every way and has added honor and luster to his family name.

From the time President Smith assumed his high office he has been a busy president. Not only has he maintained a rigorous schedule, directing the affairs of the three-million member, worldwide Church, but also he maintains a busy schedule in carrying the message of the restored gospel to members of the Church at home and abroad, in their wards and stakes, in the colleges and universities, at funerals and in other places.

It has been my privilege to accompany President and Sister Smith as they have traveled about the Church since he became President. I have observed the great love that the people, young and old, have for him, and I have seen him reciprocate by leaving a blessing upon the people. I have watched as he has picked up little children and held them in his arms and have seen the tenderness with which he has greeted them. As he left the Tabernacle at a recent general conference, a little girl ran up to him, and after picking her up and embracing her, he returned her to a distraught aunt who had thought her to be lost. When she was asked, "Where did you go? We thought you were lost," the three-year-old replied, "I wasn't lost. I was in the arms of the Prophet."

While en route to an appointment in Southern Utah, the President saw some little children on the school grounds in a small town. He asked me to stop the car so that he and Sister Smith could visit with the children who were out for recess, and soon they gathered around to see and speak to the President and his dear wife. When some of the children ran to get the teachers and the principal, who was a stake president, they had a difficult time convincing them that President Smith was indeed sitting in a car just outside the little schoolhouse.

Although he has been so blessed that he has never really been sick, he has great compassion for those who suffer. He has sat up at night with his own children when they were young, caring for them. This was not only to comfort them, but to relieve their mother, who had had a long and strenuous day and needed the rest. When shown a picture of a group of handicapped children to whom he and Sister Smith had recently spoken and sung a duet, tears came to his eyes as he reflected upon the circumstances of these wonderful young people.

I have found the President to be forthright, honest, and a fearless defender of the faith. He has always been a kind, compassionate, and loving father and a devoted, considerate, and gentle husband and companion. To know him is to love, honor, and respect him, not only as a man and as a friend, but as the Prophet of the Lord.

—D. Arthur Haycock
Secretary to President
Joseph Fielding Smith

PREFACE

One of our most pleasant assignments as editors of the *Church News* is covering the activities and travels of President Joseph Fielding Smith. Whether he has been meeting with the Polynesian Saints in Hawaii or addressing students in Idaho or dedicating a chapel in California or counseling members in England, we have witnessed a prophet among the people. His love and genuine interest for the members of the Church is illustrated everywhere he goes.

He has traveled a great deal since becoming President as he has taken the message of the restored gospel to the members of the Church in their wards and stakes and missions.

The purpose of this book is to record, for all, the travels and highlights of speeches of President Smith—in words and with pictures—and to capture some of the warmth and love he has demonstrated as we have observed him in carrying out his responsibilities as President of the worldwide Church.

J M. Heslop
Dell R. Van Orden

ACKNOWLEDGMENTS

Grateful appreciation is expressed to the management of the *Deseret News* for providing the opportunity to write this book through our experiences in covering the activities and travels of President Joseph Fielding Smith.

Our thanks to those who are close to President Smith, particularly his personal secretary, D. Arthur Haycock, for sharing experiences and assisting in the interviews with the President.

Photo credits are gratefully given to the *Deseret News* photographers and the *Church News* staff.

TABLE OF CONTENTS

Page

President Harold B. Lee, at rostrum, leads members of the First Presidency in sustaining vote of their quorum at solemn assembly in the Salt Lake Tabernacle.

1

*"No man of himself can lead
this church. It is the Church of
the Lord Jesus Christ;
he is at the head."*

A New President Sustained

President Joseph Fielding Smith, who was ordained and
set apart January 23, 1970, as President of The Church of
Jesus Christ of Latter-day Saints, was sustained by the
membership of the Church in solemn assembly in the Salt
Lake Tabernacle on April 6, 1970—exactly 140 years to the
day since the Church was restored by his great-uncle,
the Prophet Joseph Smith.

The solemn assembly was the first such assembly since
the one held in April, 1951, when David O. McKay was
sustained as President. The procedure for sustaining President Smith followed the same pattern that was established
when John Taylor was sustained as President in 1880, and
that had been used ever since when a new President of
the Church was sustained.

The priesthood of the Church was seated by quorums,
occupying the entire main floor of the Tabernacle. The
First Presidency, the Council of Twelve, and all other
General Authorities occupied their usual places on the
Tabernacle rostrum. Other groups of the priesthood—
namely, patriarchs, high priests, seventies, elders, priests,
teachers, and deacons—were seated in designated places on
the main floor. The general membership of the Church was
seated in the balcony.

Voting procedure was by separate quorums of the

1

priesthood first and then by the general assembly, including the priesthood. This special voting was for the First Presidency, the Council of Twelve, and the Patriarch to the Church. After these officers were sustained, the rest of the General Authorities and the general officers of the Church were presented for sustaining vote in the manner followed in a regular general conference.

I stand before you today in humility and in thanksgiving, grateful for the blessings which the Lord has poured out upon me, upon my family, upon you, and upon all his people. I know we are engaged in the work of the Lord and that he raises up men to do his work in every time and age of the earth's history.

As a church and as a people, we have been greatly blessed for many years by the inspired leadership, the great spiritual insight, and the firm hand of President David O. McKay. Now that his valiant work here is finished and he has been called home to serve in other ways, the Lord has given the reigns of responsibility and leadership in his earthly kingdom to others of us who remain.

And since we know the Lord "giveth no commandments unto the children of men, save he shall prepare a way for them that they may accomplish the thing which he commandeth them," we are most humbly confident that under his guidance and direction this work will continue to prosper.

I desire to say that no man of himself can lead this church. It is the Church of the Lord Jesus Christ; he is at the head. The Church bears his name, has his priesthood, administers his gospel, preaches his doctrine, and does his work. He chooses men and calls them to be instruments in his hands to accomplish his purposes, and he guides and directs them in their labors. But men are only instruments in the Lord's hands, and the honor and glory for all that his servants accomplish is and should be ascribed unto him forever.

If this were the work of man, it would fail, but it is the work of the Lord, and he does not fail. And we have the assurance that if we keep the commandments and are valiant in the testimony of Jesus and are true to every trust, the Lord will guide and direct us and his church in the paths of righteousness, for the accomplishments of all his purposes.

Our faith is centered in the Lord Jesus Christ, and through him in the Father. We believe in Christ, accept him as the Son of God, and have taken his name upon us in the waters of baptism, and are his sons and his daughters by adoption.

I rejoice in the work of the Lord and glory in the sure knowledge I have in my soul of its truth and divinity!

President Richard M. Nixon, flanked by members of the First Presidency, addresses huge crowd from steps of Church Office Building on July 24, 1970.

Children have always had a special place in President Smith's heart. Here, after leaving ward house in Ephraim, Utah, President Smith gives young admirer a big hug.

2

President Smith loves to be
among the people. "The thing that
has been most satisfying over
the years is meeting so many people
who are true and faithful to
their covenants."

"In the Arms of the Prophet"

President Joseph Fielding Smith loves to be among the people.

"The thing that has been most satisfying over the years," President Smith has said, "is meeting so many people who are true and faithful to their covenants. They are so friendly, wanting to shake hands and express their love. I meet wonderful members wherever I go."

President Smith's warm welcome is extended to crowds who gather to greet him or to a friend on the street.

Shaking hands with a small girl, he may chide her for chewing gum or politely question her about her studies in school.

President Smith took great delight in speaking a few words of greeting in Spanish and exchanging an "*abrazo*" in the true Mexican style in May, 1970, when a group of Church members traveled by bus from Monte Corona Branch to meet him. None of the Mexican group spoke English; they were humble farm

families, but the exchange was warm and the spirit
wonderful.

The President will sing along with a group of
Hawaiian volleyball players in Salt Lake City for
the All-Church tournament, or he will talk quietly
in his office with an old friend.

He enjoys having lunch with his sons. He is pleased
to shake hands with youth from Moses Lake, Wash-
ington, or attend a banquet with the members of a
Salt Lake City stake. Perhaps most of all, he enjoys
meeting with the brethren with whom he works.

President Smith is never late for a meeting, often-
times arriving several minutes early. It is not un-
common for him to be seated on the stand well
ahead of the starting time for a meeting or fireside.

Following general conference in April, 1970, when
President Smith was sustained, a large crowd gathered
at the door of the Tabernacle anxious to get a glimpse
of him.

From the crowd, wriggling between legs, came a
small girl who made her way to President Smith.
Soon she was in his arms for a big hug. Quickly a
Deseret News photographer snapped a picture, and just
as quickly the little girl disappeared back into the
crowd.

The picture, unidentified, appeared in the Church
News. The little girl was not unidentified to her proud
grandmother, Mrs. Milo Hobbs of Preston, Idaho, who
promptly sent a letter to President Smith to share the
information.

"I am so happy to identify the little girl as our
granddaughter, Venus Hobbs. She has a birthday on
April 17, when she will be four years old," Grandmother Hobbs wrote.

On her birthday, little Venus Hobbs, who lives in
Torrance, California, received a surprise telephone
call from President and Sister Smith, who were spend-

ing the week in California. They sang "Happy Birthday" over the phone to her. Venus was delighted at the song, and her parents were touched with tears to think the President of the Church would call.

It was explained that Venus had been with two aunts at conference but had slipped away. They feared that she was lost among the crowd, and when she returned they asked, "How did you get lost?"

"I wasn't lost!" she said.

"Who found you?" they asked.

"I was in the arms of the Prophet," she replied.

President Smith loves children. Wherever he goes, he takes great delight in shaking their hands and greeting them.

President Smith ponders question before giving answer during press conference, held the day after he became President.

8

3

*"The time will come
when the truth of
the gospel will
cover the earth."*

President Smith Meets the Press

The day after President Smith was ordained and set apart as President of the Church, the First Presidency held a press conference on January 24, 1970, in the Church Office Building. About 25 newspaper, radio, and television reporters and cameramen surrounded the large table in the First Presidency room. The questions had been submitted in advance, and they were read and answered by the brethren in this meeting.

President Harold B. Lee, first counselor in the First Presidency, introduced the conference by making the following statement: "Gentlemen and Ladies, President Smith has asked me to ask the questions that you have submitted, and may I first say that we welcome you here, and we trust that we can clarify some of the questions that you have had in your minds as you present them to President Smith and his counselors in this reorganization."

Following are some of the questions answered by President Smith:

Question: President Smith, what do you see as the future of the LDS Church?

President Smith: I think the Lord has given the answer to that. The time will come when the truth of the gospel will cover the earth. Christ will come in his own due time to reign upon the earth, and at that time everything will be set in order. Now, as I understand this, there will be some wonderful changes in the earth, and troubles among the people who will not repent and keep the commandments of the Lord.

Question: Many denominations have reported decreased attendance during the past decade, especially among the young. The Mormon Church is known for its strong programs for youth. Have you seen any decline in interest among the young in recent years in the Mormon faith? If not, how have you managed to hold their interest?

President Smith: I do have confidence in the youth of the Church, and we have in the Church by revelation and commandment for the benefit of the youth of Zion organizations that have been formed for the building up and strengthening of the faith of the youth of Zion. These organizations are doing a wonderful work. We have our Sunday School, as you know, and our Mutual Improvement organizations; the sisters have an organization for themselves. Our people are constantly in touch with the fundamental truths of the gospel of Jesus Christ.

Question: Do you foresee any changes in administrative practices for the growing worldwide Church?

President Smith: I think everything has been revealed in the revelations of the Lord pertaining to the preaching of the gospel and the building up of his kingdom upon the face of the earth preparatory to his coming.

Question: What do you see as your responsibilities now as the leader of nearly three million Mormons?

President Smith: My responsibility is what my responsibility has always been: to live in true accord with the fundamental principles of the gospel of Jesus Christ.

Question: President Smith, what responsibility do you feel to the thousands of members in the Church around the world who are now praying for your well-being and inspiration?

President Smith: I feel that my responsibility is to be just as faithful and true to the covenants and to the obligations as it is possible for me to be. The prayers of the Saints are in my behalf, and I know that many of them are praying not only for me, but for the other General Authorities of the Church, and I honor the members of the Church who are faithful and true. In my prayers, I ask

the Lord to bless them and to be with the members
of this church and to help to build them up and
strengthen them in the keeping of his commandments.

Question: A contemporary biography quotes Joseph
Smith as saying there are "revelations of God,
revelations of man and revelations of the devil."
Do you also believe this? If so, how do you distinguish from which source a revelation has oc-
curred?

President Smith: Sometimes, maybe, it would be a
little difficult to distinguish, but I think if we live
as we should, as Latter-day Saints, keeping the
commandments of the Lord, we have a right to
the guidance of the Holy Ghost, and if we will
follow what the Lord has commanded us to do,
that Spirit will be our companion to direct, to
give counsel, and to benefit every member of the
Church.

Question: One leader in The Church of Jesus Christ of
Latter-day Saints has said that many people
feel "prayer is old, obsolete, and a thing of the
past; however, it really is new, a thing of the
present and a thing of the future." Would you
please comment?

President Smith: The Lord has demanded (maybe I
should not use the word *demanded*, but requested)

by revelation that members of his church should be humble and diligent in his service and that they should keep his commandments and walk humbly in the light of his truth with emphasis on prayer, and that is declared so definitely in the Book of Mormon. The Book of Mormon has been given unto us by revelation, and the counsel given to those who lived here anciently is just as good, and just as true, and just as needful today as it was when their prophets received the revelations from the Lord and Savior Jesus Christ.

Question: What is the future of the LDS Church in a society that many term as moving farther and farther away from God?

President Smith: The future of the Church: The Lord has so arranged this church that every male member has some responsibility or should have in the priesthood. They begin as children, as deacons. As they grow, they advance in that priesthood and become teachers and then priests. Every member of this church is supposed to be acquainted with the fundamental truths of the gospel and a teacher therein. The Lord has made that definitely clear in the revelations given to the Prophet Joseph Smith. My duty is to seek knowledge and understanding. The Doctrine and Covenants has a section in it—maybe I should say more than one section in it—that gives us the understanding and impresses upon us the need of faithfulness, integrity, obedience, and the declaration of his truth as we mingle with our fellowmen.

An autograph in a book written by President Smith is a priceless possession.
President Smith has written 25 books.

4

President Smith usually
has a pleasant smile and a few
quips for newsmen.

"The Camera Snapped"

One of the first official acts of the First Presidency after President Joseph Fielding Smith was set apart as President was to hold a press conference.

Although President Smith is perhaps a bit reluctant to have his picture taken by the press, he usually has a pleasant smile and a few quips for the newsmen.

"Your camera just broke," President Smith told one photographer.

Looking at his camera, the photographer replied, "Oh, no, you didn't break the camera, President Smith."

"But I heard it snap," the President replied.

"Just one more!" is the photographers' byword.

"How come just one more?" President Smith asks.

"Perhaps the next one will be the best picture," is the reply.

"I don't know what you do with all the pictures, I never see that many printed," he says with a smile that just may make that "the best picture."

Although he enjoys people, President Smith does not like to be fussed over. He likes the simple, sincere expressions. He likes to be independent and do for himself. He likes to be alone and to study.

"Every member of the Church is supposed to be acquainted with the fundamental truths of the gospel and be a teacher therein. The scriptures impress upon us the need for faithfulness, integrity, and obedience, and the declaration of his truth as we mingle with our fellowmen," he has said.

President Smith has shared his love for the scriptures and his knowledge of them with his fellowmen. Among his writings of 25 books are five entitled *Answers to Gospel Questions.*

When asked a scriptural question, he would be most likely to respond with, "Do you have your Bible?"

He likes his questioners to read it as it is recorded, and with a reference he directs them to the proper scripture.

One student was heard to say, referring to President Smith, "Oh, he knows them all by heart."

On one occasion several years ago, President Smith could not find the standard works as he was speaking from the pulpit in a ward. He presented scriptures and his message without the books, but the next day he bought a set and sent them to the ward.

His interest in the scriptures goes back to his childhood, when he was taught the value of the word of the Lord. When he was ten years old, he would find a comfortable spot in the hay loft and read the Book of Mormon. Outside would be the noise of a ball game where the other children of the neighborhood would be at play.

Later he served as secretary to his father, Joseph F. Smith, the sixth President of the Church. This closeness to the scriptures, an understanding of their importance, and the natural instinct to "look it up" have contributed to his desire to share the messages of the scriptures.

The 25 books written by President Smith are dedicated to bringing the teachings of the gospel to the people of the world and to increasing the understanding of the members of the Church.

President Smith, who types with a style of his own, spends many hours at his typewriter, writing the material in his books. "I have written them all with these two hands," he has said. A new typewriter and desk have replaced his old roll-back typewriter desk with folding leaves. He still has a typewriter in his office.

Reading has always been part of his life. "I read most everything that is good. I like history, geography, current events, and, of course, Church books," he says.

"The standard works of the Church should be in the home someplace convenient to all the members of the family, not on the top shelf of the bookcase."

5

"My ancestors came here
in the early days to
find a place where
they could worship the
Lord according to the dictates
of their own consciences."

A Proud Heritage

President Smith was awarded an honorary life membership in the Sons of Utah Pioneers May 1, 1970, at the annual banquet of chapter presidents and directors of the national organization at Pioneer Village in Salt Lake City.

Eugene P. Watkins, Salt Lake City, national president, presented President Smith with a life membership pin and certificate. He was the third consecutive Church President so honored by the SUP; Presidents David O. McKay and George Albert Smith were previously honored.

I am proud of my pioneer heritage. My father, President Joseph F. Smith, walked across the plains as a young boy. My ancestors, as well as yours, came here in the early days to find a place where they could worship the Lord according to the dictates of their own consciences, and where they could work out their own salvation with fear and trembling before the Lord.

We are so far removed from our pioneer forebears that the record of their service and sacrifice sometimes becomes dim in our minds. We do not realize all that they went through—their hardships, their sufferings, the persecutions, the murders, the drivings that came upon them before they started on their westward journey—and yet they arrived in this valley rejoicing. It was President George A. Smith who was responsible for the statement that they came here of their own free will and choice—because they had to; and that is true.

They crossed the plains, many of them pushing handcarts containing the meager possessions that they had. They traveled the weary miles with sore and bleeding feet, through hardships and suffering that we do not understand, and arrived in this valley of the Salt Lake, and were grateful to the Lord that he had preserved their lives and brought them to a place of peace where they could worship; and all this, if you please, because they loved the truth.

President Smith dons hard hat for ceremony at cornerstone laying of Provo Temple.

6

*"In this mortal sphere,
we all have weaknesses. None
of us has physical perfection.
These things are part of
the trials and tests
of mortality."*

"Does the Journey Seem Long?"

Some 200 handicapped seminary students from throughout the western United States had the rare privilege of receiving a message of comfort from President Smith on May 2, 1970. He spoke to the handicapped youths at a seminar at the Institute of Religion at the University of Utah in Salt Lake City.

Many of the young people could not hear, others could not see, some could not talk, while still others could not walk. For those who could not hear, interpreters relayed the message to them by the use of sign language.

After the President's speech, he and Sister Smith sang a duet, "Does the Journey Seem Long?" This is an original song composed by President Smith.

May I remind you that we are all children of our Father in heaven, and that we lived with him as members of his family before we were born into this world. In that life, none of us were handicapped by the various physical weaknesses and deformities that befall so many of us here in this mortal life.

However, our Eternal Father, in his great wisdom and because of his love for us, created this earth as

20

a place where we might come and gain mortal bodies and undergo the experiences of mortality. These experiences could not have been gained in any other way, and are for our benefit and blessing.

In this mortal sphere, we all have weaknesses. None of us has physical perfection. Some of us are limited in one way and some in another. I have never had as good eyesight as most people. The only differences between us are that some of us have one weakness and some another and that some of us are more severely handicapped than others.

These things are part of the trials and tests of mortality. As a matter of fact, in one of the revelations the Lord says: "I give unto men weakness that they may be humble; and my grace is sufficient for all men that humble themselves before me."

The important thing in life is not how well off we are physically, but how strong and well we are spiritually. I am sure we all understand that in the resurrection all men will have physical perfection. None of the handicaps of mortality will remain with us in that day when we come forth from the grave.

And so our real concern in life becomes one of being humble and faithful and of keeping the commandments so we shall be entitled to the blessings of full salvation in the world to come.

It is my sincere prayer that the Lord will bless all of us, each one in his or her circumstances, so that eventually every good blessing, both temporally and spiritually, may be ours.

And I plead with you to do the best you can in all things, under the circumstances in which you find yourselves, and if you do this, it will be all the Lord expects of you.

Oscar W. McConkie, Jr., president of University Second Stake in Salt Lake City, conducts LDSSA meeting honoring President Smith.

7

"Salvation comes by belief in the Lord and in his prophets."

Guided by Prophets

Eight thousand University of Utah students paid tribute to President Smith May 3, 1970, at the annual spring fireside of the Latter-day Saints Student Association in the Salt Lake Tabernacle on Temple Square.

Themed "Take Heed to Yourselves," the fireside featured a number of tributes to the President. A large portrait, painted by an LDSSA member, was displayed before the capacity congregation.

All my life, from my youngest days, I have felt to thank the Lord that he has called prophets in this day to lead and guide his people in paths of truth and righteousness, and to warn the world of the calamities that will befall them unless they repent and accept the gospel.

I was born when President Brigham Young was still alive, and from the days of my youth to the present time have had the privilege of sitting at the feet of the prophets, of hearing their testimonies of the divinity of this great work, and of feeling the good spirit that comes from those who are in tune

23

with the Holy Ghost and who receive guidance from the Lord.

The great men who have presided over this church in past days and who have directed its affairs as they in turn were guided by the Lord have truly been the servants of the Most High. I rejoice in walking in their footsteps and in following the course they have charted.

When Joseph Smith was asked about his prophetic calling, he responded, somewhat modestly, by saying that he was a prophet and so also were all those who had the testimony of Jesus, which is the spirit of prophecy. This puts me in mind of the great cry of the Prophet Moses: "Would God that all the Lord's people were prophets, and that the Lord would put his spirit upon them."

Nearly 40 years ago, I wrote in my book *The Way to Perfection* the following:

"A prophet is one who has the inspiration of the Holy Spirit; one who can testify from revelation that Jesus Christ is the Son of God. He is one who is faithful in that knowledge and one who magnifies the authority placed upon him.

"Every man who can say knowingly that Jesus Christ is the Son of God, and the Savior of men, is a prophet. This knowledge comes only through the testimony of the Holy Spirit. Men may believe Jesus to be the Christ, but to know it requires revelation from the Holy Ghost. Every man, therefore, who has the guidance of the Holy Ghost, and magnifies his priesthood, is a prophet."

Now, I think that above all else in the world I, and you, and all members of the Church should seek to be guided by the Spirit of the Lord. To the extent that we gain the guidance of that Spirit we will be prophets to ourselves and in our own affairs, and we will also find ourselves in harmony with those prophets whom the Lord has placed in the First Presidency and in the Council of the Twelve to guide and direct the affairs of his kingdom on earth.

Joseph Smith taught that man is saved no faster than he gains knowledge of Jesus Christ and the saving truths of the gospel, and that no man can be saved in ignorance of these things. Salvation comes by belief in the Lord and in his prophets. It comes to those who gain the companionship of the Spirit and become prophets in their own right. It comes to those who love the Lord and who keep his commandments.

The Reverend M. A. Givens, escorted by Presiding Bishop John H. Vandenberg, renews acquaintances with President and Sister Smith during "Good Samaritan" banquet in June, 1970.

8

*"The commandment to keep
records is just as valid
and essential today
as it was in the days of Adam
and down through history."*

The Keeper of Records

At a dinner in the Lion House in Salt Lake City on June
29, 1970, employees of the Church Historian's Office paid
tribute to President Smith—a man who devoted 64 years of
service in the Historian's Office. Filmed glimpses of President Smith were shown, depicting various activities of his
years of service.

I suppose all my life I've had an interest in Church
history. I have read through and through every volume
of Church history. The Church is a living organism,
and the Lord has commanded since the beginning of
time that records be kept. Did you ever stop to consider what an awful condition the world would be in
if no one had been inspired to keep records?

The commandment to keep records is just as valid
and essential today as it was in the days of Adam and
down through history. My grandfather, the brother
of the Prophet Joseph Smith, was appointed to keep
the records of this dispensation. And from that day
on, it has been vital to keep records in the Church.

As you know, more than half my life has been

spent as the Church Historian. From 1921 to the first of this year, I occupied the same office in the southwest corner of the third floor of the Church Office Building. It has been quite an adjustment for me to get used to stopping off on the first floor rather than taking the elevator to the third floor. I began working in the old Historian's Office across the street when I became Assistant Church Historian in 1906. We then moved into the present office in 1917.

Meeting with you tonight under these circumstances brings back a flood of memories of those 64 years in the Historian's Office of the Church. I appreciate you good people and thank you for your devotion, your service, and your loyalty to the Church and to the cause of gathering and recording important historical facts as an official part of the records of the Church.

Working at his typewriter is a familiar activity for President Smith, who typed the manuscripts for all his books.

9

"We believe in the dignity
and divine origin of man.
Our faith is founded on
the fact that God is our
Father and we are his children."

South of the Border

The first President of the Church to visit Mexico in 25 years was President Joseph Fielding Smith, who spent a week there in July, 1970. When he arrived at the airport in Mexico City, thousands of grateful Saints were there to greet him. As he walked up the concourse, the members burst into a spontaneous singing in Spanish of "We Thank Thee, O God, for a Prophet."

While in Mexico City, President Smith addressed two stakes in conference sessions the afternoon of July 12, 1970; he spoke to 2,500 persons at the Mexico City Stake at two o'clock and to 2,700 at the Mexico City North Stake at five o'clock. At both conference sessions, interpreters translated for him as he spoke.

Both stake centers were filled to overflowing. After each meeting the President's car weaved through the massive crowds on the parking lots, as members waved good-bye and reverently bid him *"adios."*

The visit to Mexico was President Smith's first trip outside the continental United States after becoming President in January, 1970.

My feelings are to bless you, and to pray our Father in heaven to look down upon you in love and mercy and give you those things which you need both temporally and spiritually.

I have been to Mexico many times, but on this visit I am especially pleased to see the great growth and progress that have come to the Church in your country. When I first came here many years ago, there was just one small mission. Now we have five missions and several stakes in the Republic of Mexico, with many thousands of members. Thousands more are being baptized each year. We now have a Church school where hundreds of your children attend.

But, brethren and sisters, with all the growth there is in the missions, the stakes, and the Church school, there is still much for all of us to do. Although we rejoice in having several thousand members of the Church in Mexico, remember that there are nearly eight million souls living in Mexico City alone who do not have the gospel.

There is much work ahead of us. The field is white, all ready to harvest. Not only must the stake and full-time missionaries be ever diligent in sharing the gospel, but all of us should be missionaries by setting a proper example and living lives worthy of emulation, thus letting our light so shine before men that others seeing our good works may be led to glorify our Father which is in heaven.

May I remind you that we are all children of our Father in heaven, and that we lived with him in heaven as members of his family before we were born into this world. Our Eternal Father, in his great wisdom and because of his love for us, created this earth as a place where we might come and gain mortal bodies and undergo experiences of mortality.

These experiences could not have been gained in any other way, and are for our benefit and blessing. Our real concern in life is one of being humble and faithful and of keeping the commandments so we shall be entitled to the blessings of full salvation in the world to come.

President Smith travels a great deal of the time, flying to various cities for speaking engagements, other activities.

I think if all men knew and understood who they are, and were aware of the divine source from whence they came, and of the infinite potential that is part of their inheritance, they would have feelings of kindness and kinship for each other that would change their whole way of living and that would bring peace on earth.

We believe in the dignity and divine origin of man. Our faith is founded on the fact that God is our Father and we are his children, and that all men are brothers and sisters in the same eternal family.

The God we worship is a glorified being of flesh and bones in whom all power and perfection dwell, and he has created man in his own image and likeness, with those characteristics and attributes that he himself possesses. And so our belief in the dignity and destiny of man is an essential part both of our theology and of our way of life.

It is the very basis of our Lord's teaching that the first great commandment is:

"Thou shalt love the Lord thy God with all thy heart, and with all thy soul, and with all thy mind," and the second great commandment is like unto it: "Thou shalt love thy neighbour as thyself."

Because God is our Father, we have a natural desire to love and serve him and to be worthy members of his family. We feel an obligation to do what he would have us do, to keep his commandments and live in harmony with the standards of the gospel—all of which are essential parts of true worship.

And because all men are our brothers, we have a desire to love and bless and fellowship them—and this, too, we accept as an essential part of true worship.

Thus, everything we do in the Church centers around the divine law that we are to love and worship God and love and serve our fellowmen.

Cornerstone of the Ogden (Utah) Temple, containing historical items, is laid as President Smith observes.

10

*"Temple building and temple
ordinances are at the very
heart of our religion."*

Builders of Temples

The first cornerstone-laying ceremony of a temple in
Utah since the Manti Temple cornerstone was laid in 1879
was held September 7, 1970, in Ogden, under the direction of President Smith.

About 6,000 persons attended the outdoor ceremony—
held under pleasant skies, after two days of rain—and
heard President Smith speak on the importance of temple
building.

Groundbreaking for the Ogden Temple was held in
September, 1969, and completion was scheduled for the
fall of 1971. The temple district includes 27 stakes.

I rejoice in the fact that today we are laying the
cornerstone for another temple, another house of the
Lord, another sacred place where the Saints can perform those ordinances which prepare men for exaltation in the kingdom of God.

In the early days of this dispensation, the Lord
commanded the Saints to build temples and to do it
by the tithing and the sacrifices of the people. This
is the pattern we still follow. We use the tithes of

33

the Church in temple building and we invite the
Saints in the area where a temple is to be built to
contribute of their means in its construction.

We are a temple-building people, and this is one
of the things that sets us apart from the world and
that enables us to find favor in the eyes of the Lord.
Temple building and temple ordinances are at the very
heart of our religion. Everything that the Lord has
given us centers in and is based on the atoning sacrifice of the Son of God. Because of the atonement we
gain immortality and have the opportunity so to live
that we shall be saved in the kingdom of God.

This high salvation we seek is eternal life. It
consists in the continuation of the family unit in
eternity, and it is in and through the ordinances of
the temple that eternal family units are created.

Even before the Church was organized and before
the Book of Mormon was translated, the Lord began
to reveal the glorious truths about temples and the
ordinances which would be performed in them.

What is the purpose of temples? They are holy
sanctuaries in which the ordinances of exaltation are
performed. They are houses of the Lord in which we
can be married for time and for all eternity and have
our children sealed to us, so that if we are faithful
and true in all things the family unit shall continue
in eternity. And one of the most glorious things
about it is that these sealing blessings are available
also, on a vicarious basis, for our progenitors who
died without a knowledge of the gospel.

Thus, we have one of the greatest privileges of
service that has ever come to any people. We can
build temples to open the door so that our worthy
ancestors may inherit like blessings with us in the
kingdom of God. There is no more glorious work than
the perfecting of family units through the ordinances
of the house of the Lord.

Now, we are all engaged in this great work. The Lord's hand is in it. This temple is being built because the Lord wants it built, and when it is finished we shall dedicate it to him, and it will be his house. And added souls will be saved because we have served and sacrificed in this way.

I think we should strive with great zeal to prepare our children for temple marriage and then to keep the covenants made incident to that holy order of matrimony. And I have full confidence that if we go forward in faith and devotion on the Lord's errand, he will bless us in this and in all respects.

Wherever President Smith goes, he is greeted by huge crowds. Thousands turn out to hear and see him as he travels around the Church.

Boy Scouts keep crowd back as President Smith walks from street to Oahu Stake Center in Laie for conference address.

11

*"The responsibility to bring
up children in light
and truth is one that
rests upon the parents."*

The Heavens Smile

"The heavens smile over Laie because of the presence
of the Prophet, the mouthpiece of God." This tribute, given
in Hawaiian in honor of President Smith as he visited
Laie, Oahu, Hawaii, September 11 to September 19, 1970,
epitomized the heartwarming reception given him by
thousands of Polynesian Saints.

Everywhere he went, he received the love and respect
of the islanders, a people so close to the hearts of the
Smith family. It was President Smith's father, Joseph F.
Smith, sixth President of the Church, who played a leading role in the permanent establishment of Laie, now rich
in Mormon history and tradition, more than 80 years ago.

President Smith spoke at the largest stake conference
gathering in the history of the Oahu Stake on September
13, 1970, in Laie. A total of 3,245 persons filled the chapel,
cultural hall, hallways, entrance ways, and overflow rooms,
connected to the chapel by closed-circuit television. Members started arriving as early as 5:00 A.M. By 7:30, two
and a half hours before the meeting was to start, the building was filled.

President Smith was deeply touched at the close of
the meeting as the congregation arose and sang "Aloha
Oe," the traditional farewell song in Hawaii.

As members of the Church, all of us have certain obligations. The responsibility to bring up children in light and truth is one that rests upon the parents. It is to parents that the Lord speaks when he commands that children should be taught faith, repentance, baptism, and the laying on of hands for the gift of the Holy Ghost, with the decree that if we do this, we will be blessed. If we fail, the sin will be upon the shoulders of the parents.

We are all children of our Father in heaven, and we lived with him in heaven as members of his family before we were born into this world. Our Eternal Father, in his great wisdom and because of his love for us, created this earth as a place where we might come and gain mortal tabernacles and undergo experiences pertaining to mortal life. These experiences could not have been gained in any other way, and are for our blessing.

Our real concern in life is one of being humble and faithful and of keeping the commandments so we shall be entitled to the blessings of full salvation in the world to come. I think if all men knew and understood who they are, and were aware of the divine source from whence they came and of the infinite potential that is part of their inheritance, they would have feelings of kindness and kinship for each other which bring peace on earth.

Our belief in the dignity and destiny of man is an essential part of our theology given to the Church in this mortal life.

Because God is our Father, we have a natural desire to love and serve him and to be worthy members of his family. We feel an obligation to do what he would have us do, to keep his commandments and live in harmony with the standards of the gospel— all of which is an essential part of true worship. Thus, everything we do in the Church centers around the divine law that we are to love and worship God and love and serve our fellow beings.

I have a great concern for the spiritual and moral welfare of our youth. Honesty, sincerity, virtue, and freedom from sin—these are and must be basic to our way of life, if we are to realize the purpose of life.

I plead with you fathers and mothers to teach personal purity by precept and example and to counsel your children in all things. I pray that parents everywhere may be a light unto their children and that they may guide them in paths of truth and righteousness, and I pray that the children may respond to the teachings of their parents and be preserved from the evils of the world.

President Smith
loves life and
enjoys a smile.

President and Sister Smith enjoy special performance of native dances and songs at Polynesian Cultural Center during week-long visit to Hawaii.

12

*"We are expected to read
the signs of the times and to
prepare ourselves
for the Second Coming."*

When Will He Come?

President Smith's visit to Hawaii was a result of an invitation by the Church College of Hawaii to officially launch the fifteenth anniversary of its founding.

He was the fourth consecutive Church President to visit the village of Laie on the north shore of Oahu.

On September 15, 1970, he addressed 1,590 students, faculty members and guests in a devotional assembly, the official anniversary ceremony. He spoke on the second coming of Christ.

During his whirlwind visit of the island, he and Sister Smith also toured the Polynesian Cultural Center, met with missionaries attending the Language Training Mission in Laie and with missionaries of the Hawaii Mission in Honolulu, and were honored at receptions, luncheons, and dinners.

As the Hawaiian visit neared its end, President Smith expressed appreciation to the Hawaiian members: "Words cannot express our appreciation for your kindness. We'll never forget you."

I have been asked many times if I know when the Lord will come, when the Son of Man will return to usher in the millennial era and bring peace to the earth.

Oh, yes, we know this is the Saturday night of time, that this is the sixth day drawing to the close, and that the Lord will come in the morning of the Sabbath, or seventh day, of the earth's temporal existence. We know that he will come to inaugurate the millennial reign and to take his rightful place as King of kings and Lord of lords, to rule and reign on the earth, as it is his right to do.

But we must do more than give lip service to this doctrine which teaches us that the coming of the Son of Man will be tomorrow.

The Second Coming will be a day of sorrow or rejoicing, a day of gladness or anguish, a day of burning or salvation, a day of vengeance or redemption—it all depends upon the individual. If we keep the commandments and walk in the light, we shall abide the day and find peace with the Lord; but if we walk in worldly paths, we shall be burned as stubble and cast out with the wicked.

We are expected to read the signs of the times and to prepare ourselves for the Second Coming. The Lord has said, "And whoso treasureth up my word shall not be deceived." We know that we live in the age or dispensation when he shall return, but the actual time remains hidden, and I think the Lord leaves us in doubt for a wise purpose. He wants to encourage us to be ready at all times.

As far as the world is concerned, he will come "as a thief in the night," which means he will come without warning and even when they least expect it.

And even where the saints, his elect people, are concerned, though they shall be able to read the signs of the times and "shall know that he is near, even at the doors," yet he says to them: "But of that day, and hour, no man knoweth; no, not the angels of God in heaven, but my Father only."

Now, I believe that the coming of the Son of God is not far away—how far I do not know. We are living in the last days; these are the days when the signs of the times are being fulfilled. Much that has been promised by the prophets to precede the Second Coming has already taken place.

But there are some other things that the prophets spoke about that are now transpiring and that we can recognize, but that have not wholly been fulfilled. These things are the wars and perplexities that shall cover the earth during the Saturday of time.

In this present day, confusion, bloodshed, misery, plague, famine, earthquake, and other calamities shall cover the face of the earth.

The distress and perplexity, bloodshed and terror, selfish ambition of despotic rulers, such as the world has never seen before—all indicate that the great and dreadful day of the Lord is near, even at our doors.

Elder Boyd K. Packer of the Council of Twelve pays tribute to President Smith during President's Honor Night in Ogden, Utah.

13

*"I know that the work is true,
and that it shall triumph
over all obstacles and roll
forward until the gospel
cause covers the earth as the
waters cover the mighty deep."*

The Lord's Mouthpiece

President Smith was honored October 11, 1970, as the
Prophet of God—the Lord's mouthpiece upon the earth—at
the President's Honor Night in Ogden, Utah, sponsored
by the Institute of Religion at Weber State College.

About 3,000 persons crowded into the Ogden Tabernacle, the largest congregation ever assembled in the
building, to hear Elder Boyd K. Packer of the Council of
Twelve pay tribute to President Smith and to hear President Smith bear testimony of the truthfulness of the
restored gospel.

As President Smith arrived, the huge congregation
arose and sang "We Thank Thee, O God, for a Prophet."
Elder Packer told the members, "I stand as a witness that
Joseph Fielding Smith is a prophet of God."

We are commanded to love the Lord, to love one
another, to love the truth, and to walk in paths of
virtue and holiness. The Lord expects us to honor
and respect each other and to have the spirit of unity,
harmony, and appreciation in our souls.

And the extent to which we have this spirit is the
extent to which we are living the gospel and have

45

the Spirit of the Lord. Where the Spirit of the Lord is, there is the spirit of love, of honor, and of respect for every true principle and for all good people.

Now, I extend to all of you my sincere thanks and gratitude, and I pray that the spirit of love and respect and appreciation for each other may abound in all our hearts, and that we may increase in our love of the Lord and signify this by keeping his commandments.

I know that the work is true, and that it shall triumph over all obstacles and roll forward until the gospel cause covers the earth as the waters cover the mighty deep.

I pray that we shall all be true and steadfast, and that we shall continue to enjoy the fellowship and love which the gospel brings into our lives in this life, and then go on together in eternal joy, gratitude, and love in the life to come.

One of President Smith's responsibilities, as he directs the activities of the Church, is conducting meetings. Here he is presiding at Church Expenditures Committee meeting.

Missionaries in the Language Training Mission in Provo, Utah, enjoy rare treat
of visiting with President Smith.

14

"You will be instruments in bringing many souls into his kingdom and will be rewarded with eternal life, if you are faithful in all things."

Watchmen on the Towers

Eight hundred missionaries being trained for service in 47 different missions at the Language Training Mission in Provo, Utah, were told by the President of the Church on October 18, 1970, of the importance and satisfaction of their work.

Each year about 40 percent of the 13,000 missionaries representing the Church receive training at the Provo mission center, located on the Brigham Young University campus.

There is nothing that any of you could do for the time and the season of this present appointment that would in any way compare in importance with it. In large measure the spiritual well-being and eternal destiny of the many nonmembers of the Church whose lives you will touch is also in your hands.

We are engaged in the Lord's work. We are his agents and representatives. We need his Spirit to guide us in all we undertake to do, and I pray that there may be a rich outpouring of this Spirit upon each of you during these coming years of missionary work.

The Church has two great responsibilities; that is, the members of the Church have these responsibilities. It is our individual duty to preach the gospel by precept and by example among our neighbors. It is also the responsibility of each of us individually to seek after our dead. What we are concerned with at this time is this matter of preaching the gospel to the world. It is an obligation that rests upon every member of the Church, and particularly upon those who are called and set apart to devote their full energies and strength to the missionary cause.

All people are entitled to hear the message, so this responsibility to teach the world is an outstanding one. We cannot get away from this obligation. The Lord declared that his coming is nigh at hand and that he would cut short his work in righteousness. It is our duty, then, to do all we can, and the Lord will bring to pass other forces, that his work may advance and his words be fulfilled.

We members of the Church are witnesses. That is our message to the world, and the message is sorely needed in the face of the false doctrines taught by the power of men. When men are turning from the Lord and seeking to find everlasting truth without his aid, our mission becomes all the more urgent in calling men to repentance and to a belief in the redemption brought to pass through the atonement of the Son of God, whose blood was shed for the sins of the world.

It is our message and our mission to the world to preach this truth, and to establish faith in the hearts of the people, and endeavor to get them to believe in Jesus Christ as their Redeemer and as the Son of God.

Men love darkness today rather than light, just as they did in the days of the Redeemer. They are blinded against truth and righteousness; they see it not. Yet our mission is to proclaim it and bring to repentance just as many of the children of our Father in heaven as it is possible for us to do.

We all know that the Lord is in distress because of wickedness. People in every land reject the gospel, and the judgments of the Lord have been poured out upon them. These judgments are continuing and will continue if the people will not repent. The Lord has said that he will come to set things in order when the cup of iniquity is full. The missionaries of the Church are sent out to warn the people and to gather out of the nations all who are willing to repent and receive the gospel. They are also commanded to warn others that they might escape the calamities and the judgments which are bound to continue if people will not receive the gospel.

We are watchmen on the towers of Israel. The Lord has placed in our hands great and wonderful responsibilities. No men anywhere in all the earth, no matter what their calling, hold responsibility equal to that which we have received, for we have had conferred upon us the priesthood of God.

If you keep close to the Lord, he will lead you to those who are seeking the truth. Utilize your talents and strength. Seek the Spirit of the Lord in your work, and God will bless and magnify you beyond anything you had thought possible. You will be instruments in bringing many souls into his kingdom and will be rewarded with eternal life, if you are faithful in all things.

15

*"The Lord gave commandments
that both men and women
should cover their
bodies and observe the law
of chastity at all times."*

A Plea for Modesty

In St. George, Utah, to set apart a new temple presidency, President Smith accepted an invitation to speak on November 9, 1970, to seminary and institute students of the area. About 400 young people listened to him as he urged them to be modest in dress and in actions.

When I was a boy, we had a horse named Junie. She was one of the most intelligent animals I ever saw. She seemed almost human in her ability. I couldn't keep her locked in the barn because she would continually undo the strap on the door of her stall. I used to put the strap connected to the half-door of the stall over the top of the post, but she would simply lift it off with her nose and teeth. Then she would go out in the yard.

There was a water tap in the yard used for filling the water trough for our animals. Junie would turn this one with her teeth and then leave the water running. My father would get after me because I couldn't keep that horse in the barn. She never ran away; she just turned on the water and then walked around the yard or over the lawn or through the garden. In the middle of the night, I would hear the water running, and then I would have to get up and shut if off and lock Junie up again.

We couldn't keep Junie from getting out of her stall. But that doesn't mean she was bad, because she wasn't. Father wasn't about to sell or trade her, because she had so many other good qualities that made up for this one little fault. She was as reliable and dependable at pulling our buggy as she was adept at getting out of the stall. And this was important, because Mother was a licensed midwife. When she would get called to a confinement somewhere in the valley, usually in the middle of the night, I would have to get up, take a lantern out to the barn, and hitch Junie up to the buggy. I was only about ten or eleven years old at the time, and that horse had to be gentle and yet strong enough to take me and Mother all over the valley, in all kinds of weather. One thing I never could understand, however, was why most of the babies had to be born at night and so many of them in winter.

I recount this personal experience; although it happened some years back and even though it is from another period and time, it has something in common with experiences and temptations you are now facing. I hope you know how important these truths are for you in your life.

Isaiah, one of the great prophets of early times, saw our day, and he described the conditions that would prevail in these latter days. Now, in this modern day, Isaiah's prophecy is being fulfilled.

As I walk along the streets on my way to or from the Church Office Building, I see both young and older women, many of them "daughters of Zion," who are immodestly dressed. I realize that times and fashions do change.

Still, this reminds me of a time when I was a youth attending the Salt Lake Stake Academy and later the Latter-day Saints University. The girls were dressed neatly from head to foot in shirtwaists and full skirts down to their ankles. I recall an incident that happened when a group of students—young girls and boys—took a short trip up City Creek Canyon. While doing a little hiking, one of the girls slipped and caught her dress on a limb, exposing her leg to the knee. She was so embarrassed that she wanted to withdraw from the group and return home. It took some persuasion by the other girls to have her remain and try to forget the incident.

The principle of modesty and propriety is still the same today as it was then. The standards expressed by the General Authorities of the Church are that women, as well as men, should dress modestly. They are taught proper deportment and modesty at all times. It is, in my judgment, a sad reflection on the "daughters of Zion" when they dress immodestly. Moreover, this remark pertains to the young men as well as to the young women. The Lord gave commandments that both men and women should cover their bodies and observe the law of chastity at all times.

I am making a plea for modesty and chastity and for all the members of the Church, male and female alike, to be chaste, clean in their lives, and obedient to the covenants and commandments the Lord has given us.

President Smith, with his personal secretary, D. Arthur Haycock, walks past the Lion House and Beehive House on South Temple Street in Salt Lake City.

16

*"We are all in need,
as never before, of the guiding
and preserving care
of the Lord."*

A Christmas Message

As Christmas 1970 neared—the first for President Smith as President of the Church—he issued a Christmas greeting to the members of the Church throughout the world asking that they center their faith in the Son of God and gain for themselves that peace which passeth understanding.

I greet you at this Christmas season, in love and fellowship, and with a prayer that our Eternal Father will look down upon you in mercy and pour out his bounteous blessings upon you.

In these times when iniquity abounds, when there are great tribulations on the earth, when there are wars and rumors of wars, we are all in need, as never before, of the guiding and preserving care of the Lord.

We need to know that in spite of all the troubles and ills which befall us, still the Lord is governing in the affairs on the earth, and that if we keep his commandments and are true and faithful to his laws, he will bless us here and now and reward us with eternal life in his kingdom in due course.

Those of us who know that Joseph Smith was

called of God to restore the fullness of the everlasting gospel in these, the last days, are entitled to a special feeling of peace and thanksgiving now and always.

We rejoice in the birth of the Son of God among men. We are grateful for the atoning sacrifice he worked out by the shedding of his own blood. We are thankful that he has redeemed us from death and opened the door so that we may gain eternal life.

We pray for peace on earth, for the spread of the gospel, and for the final triumph of truth. We plead with our Father's other children everywhere to join with us in doing those things which will give us all peace in this world and eternal glory in the world to come.

And now, as one who has an absolute knowledge of the truth and divinity of this great latter-day work, I bear my testimony that it is true and that we are engaged in our Father's business.

I know that Jesus Christ is the Son of God; that he died upon the cross for the sins of the world; that he rose from the dead; and that he hath brought life and immortality to light through the gospel.

I know that Joseph Smith is a prophet of God; that the gospel has been restored in this dispensation; and that The Church of Jesus Christ of Latter-day Saints is in very deed the kingdom of God on earth.

And I now pray that at this Christmas season, and at all times, we may center our faith in the Son of God and gain for ourselves that peace which passeth understanding.

President and Sister Smith walk to their seats at Utah State University Assembly Center in Logan, Utah.

17

"The God we worship has all power and all wisdom, and he knows all things."

The Glory of God Is Intelligence

President Smith warmed the hearts of a vast audience at the Utah State University Assembly Center in Logan, Utah, January 10, 1971, as he counseled nearly 10,000 students relative to their educational pursuits. Keen attention highlighted the Sunday service, which was sponsored by the Institute of Religion.

The God we worship has all power and all wisdom, and he knows all things. Speaking of himself, he said: "The glory of God is intelligence, or, in other words, light and truth," which means that the very glory of God himself consists in the truth and light that he possesses.

Then the revelation says: "Light and truth forsake that evil one. . . . And that wicked one cometh and taketh away light and truth, through disobedience, from the children of men, and because of the tradition of their fathers." Thus, we learn that the way to gain that light and truth, which is true intelligence and which is the glory of God, is to keep the commandments and walk in the paths he has ordained.

Our Father in heaven established a plan of salva-

59

tion for his spirit children. This plan is designed to enable them to advance and progress until they gain eternal life, which is the name of the kind of life God lives. This plan is to enable the children of God to become like him and have the power and wisdom and knowledge that he possesses.

The Lord Jesus Christ is the central figure in this great plan of progression and salvation. As God's Son, he brought life and immortality to light through the gospel. During his mortal ministry, he worked out his own salvation and set a perfect example for all his brethren, so that he could say to them, "Follow thou me." His life is the perfect pattern. He is the prototype of salvation.

In Section 93 of the Doctrine and Covenants, the Lord reveals that even though Christ is the Creator of worlds and the Redeemer of men, yet when he "came into the world . . . and dwelt in the flesh . . . he received not of the fulness at the first, but received grace for grace; And he received not of the fulness at first, but continued from grace to grace, until he received a fulness."

Thus, the Savior came to earth, not alone to redeem men but to overcome the world, to gain mortal experiences, to be tried and tested, as is the case with all of us. And so Paul said of him: "Though he were a Son, yet learned he obedience by the things which he suffered; And being made perfect, he became the author of eternal salvation unto all them that obey him."

Our Savior kept all of his Father's commandments, and the revelation says that after the resurrection, "he received a fulness of the glory of the Father; And he received all power, both in heaven and on earth, and the glory of the Father was with him, for he dwelt in him."

Then, in this same revelation, the Lord says to us: "If you keep my commandments you shall receive of

his fulness, and be glorified in me as I am in the Father;
therefore, I say unto you, you shall receive grace for
grace."

And so we see that our very existence—our life
both in preexistence and here in mortality, and our
life hereafter as resurrected beings—is a schooling process. From eternity to eternity, we are expected to seek
knowledge and understanding of the things of God.

The Prophet taught that no man can be saved in
ignorance of God and his laws; that men are saved no
faster than they gain knowledge of Jesus Christ and
the saving truths of his gospel; and that "whatever
principle of intelligence we attain unto in this life, it
will rise with us in the resurrection. And if a person
gains more knowledge and intelligence in this life
through his diligence and obedience than another, he
will have so much the advantage in the world to
come."

Now, I ask you to note that the knowledge and
understanding of eternal truths, of which we are here
speaking, come by revelation from God as a result of
obedience to the laws and ordinances of his gospel.
Christ did not study chemistry or physics or sociology
in the colleges of his day. Indeed, as we know them,
these subjects were neither devised nor taught in his
day.

But he did so live as to receive knowledge by revelation from the Holy Ghost, thus setting the pattern for
all of us. We are commanded to "seek learning, even
by study and also by faith." I think we should do all
we can during our student years to learn those things
which will benefit us during our mortal probations and
enable us to have the means and talents to further
the Lord's work on earth. But I think that it is far
more important to seek the things of God and be in
harmony with his eternal laws so that we may inherit
the fullness of his blessings and glory in due course.

An elk skin, containing the words of song encouraging Indians to seek an education, is given to President Smith by BYU Indian students Nora Begay, left, Jeffrey Simons, and Arliene Williams.

18

*"This plan of salvation
is family centered. It leads to
eternal life . . . and is designed
to enable us to create family
units of our own."*

A Doctrine of Love

President Smith, the only man on earth who holds the keys of Elijah, was presented the Archibald F. Bennett Genealogical Award January 12, 1971, at a devotional assembly at Brigham Young University, exemplifying the person who has done the most to further the principles of genealogy in the Church.

More than 11,000 students and faculty members filled every seat and lined the stairway aisles of the BYU Fieldhouse to see the presentation and hear President Smith speak on the doctrine of salvation. Another 3,000 students heard his message by closed-circuit radio carried to other buildings on campus.

President Smith was honored as being "a driving force to see that genealogy was recognized as a program to which we should all devote our time."

Following the assembly, he was given an original recording of "Go My Son," and an elk skin that contained the words of the song, by the tribe of Many Feathers, the Indian Club on campus. The song, written by two BYU Indian students, is based on the true story of a Navajo war chief who once told his people that education is a ladder to help reach success and happiness.

I think it would be appropriate for us on this occasion to turn our attention to this glorious doctrine of salvation for the dead. It is a doctrine that shows forth the love and mercy and justice of God in his dealings with all his children—not only those whose privilege it is to receive the gospel in this life, but all those to whom this privilege does not come but who are nonetheless precious in the Lord's sight.

As members of The Church of Jesus Christ of Latter-day Saints, we are a blessed and favored people. The Lord has restored to us the sealing power, the power to bind on earth and have our acts sealed eternally in the heavens.

This sealing power is the same divine authorization received by Peter in fullness of the Lord's promise: "I will give unto thee the keys of the kingdom of heaven: and whatsoever thou shalt bind on earth shall be bound in heaven: and whatsoever thou shalt loose on earth shall be loosed in heaven."

It was given by Elijah to the Prophet Joseph Smith and Oliver Cowdery on the third day of April in 1836 in the Kirtland Temple, and it now resides in the Church and will continue to do so to the end of time.

To understand what is involved in this modern ministry of Elijah—a prophet who was translated and taken up into heaven without tasting death, but who now is a resurrected and exalted being—we must remind ourselves of two great truths:

One is that we are the spirit children of God our Heavenly Father; that we are members of his family; that we dwelt with him for long ages in our premortal life; and that he ordained a plan of progression and salvation that would enable us, if faithful and true in all things, to advance and progress until we become like him.

This plan of salvation is family centered. It leads to eternal life, and eternal life is the name of the kind of life that God our Father lives. This plan of salvation is designed to enable us to create family units of our own that are patterned after the family of our Eternal Father.

The other great truth is that God has restored in these last days the fullness of his everlasting gospel. That is, he has revealed anew the laws and principles by comformity to which we may press forward in righteousness until we gain eternal life. And he has conferred again upon men that priesthood and those powers whereby they can be sealed up unto eternal life.

Now, eternal life consists of the continuation of the family in eternity. The sealing power restored by Elijah includes the power to bind families together forever. By virtue of this power we perform marriages in the temples that cause the family units to endure for time and all eternity. And it is this same power that reaches out to include our ancestors who did not have the opportunity to receive the gospel when they lived on earth.

The Lord has decreed that all of his spirit children, every soul who has or shall live on earth, shall have a fair and a just opportunity to believe and obey the laws of his everlasting gospel. It is obvious that only a small portion of mankind has so far heard the word of revealed truth from the voice of one of the Lord's true servants. In the wisdom and justice of the Lord, all must do so.

Those who did not have the opportunity to hear the message of salvation in this life, but who would have accepted it, with all their hearts, if such an opportunity had come to them—they are the ones who will accept it in the spirit world; they are the ones for whom we shall perform the ordinances in the temples; and they are the ones who shall, in this way, become heirs with us of salvation and eternal life.

Dorothy Nielsen, University First Stake YWMIA president, presents plaque to President Smith, honoring him for "gospel scholarship."

19

*"The most important
knowledge in the world is
gospel knowledge.
It is a knowledge of
God and his laws."*

Gospel Scholarship

The largest audience ever to meet in the University of Utah Institute of Religion complex in Salt Lake City listened to President Smith speak on gospel knowledge February 7, 1971. More than 2,000 students met at the University First Stake fireside, sponsored by the stake MIA. During the meeting, President Smith was given a plaque honoring him for gospel scholarship.

You have inquiring minds and are seeking truth in many fields. I sincerely hope your greatest search is in the realm of spiritual things, because it is through a knowledge of them that we are able to gain salvation, and to make the progress that leads to eternal life in our Father's kingdom.

The most important knowledge in the world is gospel knowledge. It is a knowledge of God and his laws, of those things which men must do to work out their salvation with fear and trembling before the Lord. One of our revelations tells us that if we are to be glorified in Christ as he is in the Father, we must

67

understand and know both how to worship and what we worship.

I now desire to call your attention to what we worship; that is, to remind you of the nature and kind of being that God is so that you may worship him in spirit and in truth and thereby gain all of the blessings of his gospel.

I am sure we all know that God is known only by revelation, that he stands revealed or remains forever unknown; and so we must go to the scriptures—not to the scientists or philosophers—if we are to learn the truth about Deity. Indeed, John's great prophecy about the restoration of the gospel, by an angel who should fly in the midst of heaven, was to occur so that men could come to a knowledge of the true God, so they could be taught: "Fear God, and give glory to him; . . . and worship him that made heaven and earth, and the sea, and the fountains of water."

In other words, beginning with the restoration of the gospel in this dispensation men once again would be called upon to worship and serve their Creator rather than the false concepts of Deity that prevailed in the world. In every age, the Lord's prophets have been called upon to combat false worship and proclaim the truth about Heavenly Father.

I know that God is our Father; that he is a being in whose image man is created; that he has a body of flesh and bones as tangible as man's; and that he is the literal and personal Father of the spirits of all men.

And I know further, as the Prophet taught in the Lectures on Faith, that he is omnipotent and omniscient; that he has all power and wisdom; and that his perfections consist in the possession of all knowledge, faith or power, justice, judgment, mercy, and truth, and, for that matter, the fullness of all godly attributes.

And I believe further, as the Prophet also taught, that if we are to have that perfect faith by which we can lay hold upon eternal life, we must believe in him as the possessor of the fullness of all these characteristics and attributes. May I say also that he is an infinite and eternal being, and as an unchangeable being, he possesses these perfected powers and attributes from everlasting to everlasting, which means from eternity to eternity.

I am very grateful that we know he is an infinite and eternal being who knows all things and has all power and whose progression consists not in gaining more knowledge or power, not in further perfecting his godly attributes, but in the increase and multiplying of his kingdoms. This also is what the Prophet taught.

In Long Beach, California, thousands of young people gather in parking lot after President Smith's speech, hoping for another glimpse of him and perhaps a chance to shake his hand.

20

*"We must not follow the
marriage practices of the world.
We have greater light than
the world has and the Lord expects
more of us."*

The True Order of Marriage

The unforgettable experience of seeing and hearing President Smith thrilled more than 13,000 young people from 46 California stakes in Long Beach on April 18, 1971.

President Smith, who spoke on the importance of celestial marriage in the huge Long Beach Arena, went to Southern California in answer to an invitation by the seminary and institute students of the area.

During the meeting, President Smith was given a special plaque "in gratitude for living a life that speaks a sermon of true example."

The Lord has given us his everlasting gospel to be a light and a standard to us, and this gospel includes his holy order of matrimony, which is eternal in nature. We should not and must not follow the marriage practices of the world. We have greater light than the world has, and the Lord expects more of us than he does of them.

We know what the true order of marriage is. We know the place of the family unit in the plan of salvation. We know that we should be married in the temple, and that we must keep ourselves clean and pure so as to gain the approving seal of the Holy Spirit of Promise upon our marriage unions.

When the Lord placed Adam and Eve in the Garden of Eden, he sealed them together as husband and wife in an eternal marriage union and commanded them to multiply and replenish the earth; thus they were able to begin the process of providing mortal bodies for the spirit children of our Father in heaven.

Now, what the Lord did for Adam and Eve, he has also offered to all those who will accept the fullness of his gospel law and live in harmony with its eternal truths. He has given us temple marriage so that we can create eternal family units of our own.

I think these blessings, which center around and grow out of the continuation of the family unit in eternity, are among the most important blessings known to man.

Love is as eternal as life, and both go on after the grave. Why would anyone who knows the Lord's law deliberately choose to marry "until death do us part" and thus let death end the family relationship?

How glorious it is to know that if we are true and faithful to the laws of this highest order of matrimony, we shall continue as husband and wife, united perfectly as one forever in celestial glory.

These are glorious concepts, and along with all the other things that have been restored in this day, they came from the Lord. They are true; they are everlasting. This whole system of revealed religion that we have received is true.

It is very apparent to all of us who read the newspapers, who listen to the news accounts on the radio, and who watch what comes over television that all too many do not hold marriage and the family unit in that respect which the Lord intends.

Many people today do not honor or respect any form of marriage. Some are unfaithful to their marriage vows and live unclean and immoral lives; some break up their homes through divorce for petty and selfish reasons; and some do not even pretend to enter into legal marriages, but simply live in immorality and have children who are conceived in sin.

We are living in an evil and wicked world. But while we are in the world, we are not of the world. We are expected to overcome the world and to live as becometh saints.

I plead with you young people to keep yourselves clean and pure so that you will be entitled to go to the house of the Lord and together with the companions of your choice enjoy all these great blessings the Lord offers to you.

President and Sister Smith enjoy quiet moment in Church-owned home at Laguna Beach, California, overlooking the Pacific Ocean.

21

"These buildings are constructed by the tithing and the sacrifice of the people so that we can use them in preaching the gospel."

A Place in Which to Worship

President Smith dedicated the Laguna Hills Ward meetinghouse April 25, 1971, in El Toro, California—a structure for which he broke ground a year earlier. The ward is located in Newport Beach Stake, the only stake in the Church that has the distinction of having within its boundaries a home of the President of the Church and a home of the President of the United States.

In 1950 the Church purchased an attractive white frame home, high on the cliffs above Emerald Bay near Laguna Beach, for the President. It was first used by President George Albert Smith and since has been used by Presidents David O. McKay and Joseph Fielding Smith.

Also located in the stake boundaries is President Richard M. Nixon's Western White House in San Clemente, about 12 miles along the coast southeast of Laguna Beach.

On Sundays, when talks or other appearances are not scheduled, President Smith usually attends church services in one of the wards in the stake.

I shall say a few words about what is involved in dedicating buildings to the Lord. These buildings are constructed by the tithing and the sacrifice of the people so that we can use them in preaching the gospel and carrying forward the various programs of the Church.

In them, we teach the gospel, perform the ordinances of salvation, learn our duties, gain the companionship of the Spirit, and partake of the gifts of the Spirit. They are truly houses of the Lord, and when we dedicate them to him, they then become his and are to be used to further his purposes on earth.

But the dedicatory prayer does not change the building itself. Rather, it commits us to use the building in the way the Lord intended; it commits us to change our way of life if such is needed. It is people who change, not buildings.

We shall present this building to the Lord as one of his houses of worship. This means we shall covenant with the Lord to use this building as a place in which to worship him in the way he has commanded. It means we shall use these beautiful facilities to carry out his work and to lead souls unto salvation in his kingdom.

To the delight of thousands, President and Sister Smith often sang duets as they traveled around the Church.

President Smith addresses graduates at Ricks College baccalaureate and pays tribute to outgoing college president.

22

"There is more sin and evil in the world now than there has been at any time since the day of Noah."

A Light Unto the World

The largest building in the Upper Snake River Valley in eastern Idaho was filled to capacity May 7, 1971, as about 5,000 persons crowded into the Ricks College Fieldhouse in Rexburg, Idaho.

President Smith gave the college's annual baccalaureate address and paid tribute to John L. Clarke, who retired after serving 27 years as Ricks president, nearly twice as long as any previous administrator.

Before he developed his theme, which unequivocally portrayed the wicked state of the world today, President Smith said that President Clarke's "service in the Church and at Ricks College was of inestimable worth."

I have said many times that we lived in a wicked, wicked world. The Lord told Joseph Smith, more than a hundred years ago, that the world was ripening in iniquity and groaning under the burden of sin and darkness. And conditions are worse today than they were then.

The ripening process has increased and will continue to do so until the second coming of the Son of

Man, until the end of the world and the ushering in 'of the millennial era of peace and righteousness.

There is more sin and evil in the world now than there has been at any time since the day of Noah, when the Lord felt disposed to destroy the world by a flood so that he could send his spirit children to earth in a better and more righteous environment.

This is the day in which Christ said that iniquity shall abound. From the revelations he has given, we know that when the cup of iniquity is full, then cometh the destruction of the wicked, which is the end of the world; then cometh the day when the vine-yard shall be cleansed by fire so that righteousness and peace may be in the hearts of all who remain to live on earth during the day of the great millennium.

We pray for the millennial advent, for the day when the Lord shall come and his will shall be done on earth as it is in heaven. But until that glorious day arrives, we must learn to live in the world without being of the world. We need not despair, how-ever, because of world conditions. It is true that there is war and rebellion and immorality and sin of every sort and that these things will remain on earth until the end of the world.

But it is also true that the Lord has restored his everlasting gospel to be a light to the world and to be a standard around which the honest in heart in every nation may rally. It is true that the Lord has set up his kingdom again on earth for the last time, as a place where those who want to forsake the world and live God-fearing and righteous lives may learn how to do so.

Our Lord himself set the example. He said: "In the world ye shall have tribulation: but be of good cheer; I have overcome the world."

To us in this dispensation the Lord said: "He that is faithful and endureth shall overcome the world."

Some of our early brethren in this dispensation had a saying, "The kingdom of God or nothing," meaning that all spiritual blessings come through the Church and kingdom of God on earth and that without this we would have nothing more than the world has.

I am so grateful that we have the gospel, that we know what the Lord's laws are, and that if we keep the commandments and do the things the Lord expects of us, we shall overcome the world and gain salvation eventually in his kingdom. We have been commanded to put first in our lives the things of his kingdom. None of us have done this as fully as we should; there is some degree of worldliness in all of us, and we overcome the world by degrees.

To aid and help us in this process of working out our salvation, the Lord has given us this counsel: "That thou mayest more fully keep thyself unspotted from the world, thou shalt go to the house of prayer and offer up thy sacraments upon my holy day; For verily this is a day appointed unto you to rest from your labors, and to pay thy devotions to the Most High."

I know we face greater problems than was the case with many of our ancestors. But the Lord has not forsaken the world, nor has he left his people without guidance and inspiration. We have the truths of salvation. We have the holy priesthood. We have the gift of the Holy Ghost, and if we live the way we know we should, the Lord will guide and direct us by the power of his Spirit.

A bashful boy is timid about shaking the outstretched hand of President Smith in Ephraim, Utah.

23

*"Our whole purpose in
life should be to do those things
which will enable
us to gain eternal life."*

Eternal Progression

President Smith was honored guest May 14, 1971, at
Snow College in Ephraim, Utah, at the first annual "Snow
Day," designed to pay tribute to Lorenzo and Erastus
Snow, after whom Snow College was named in 1900.

An example of the President's great love for children was shown as he traveled from Salt Lake City to
Ephraim. He went a little out of his way to look at an
old LDS Church house in Spring City, a few miles northeast of Ephraim. As the car went through the community,
the President noticed children at play at an elementary
school. He asked that the car be stopped. Immediately
many of the children recognized him and within moments
the car was surrounded by happy, gleeful children,
thrilled with the once-in-a-lifetime opportunity to visit
with the President of the Church.

In Ephraim, about 1,300 college students, faculty
members, and townspeople crowded into the West Ward
to hear President Smith speak on eternal progression.
Before his address, he was given a plaque in recognition
of "Snow Day," which was initiated by the Institute of
Religion on campus. The plaque said, "Thanks for living a
life worthy of receiving the Lord's revelations to the
children of the world."

We have come together today to worship the Lord
and to honor two of the great spiritual giants of this
dispensation—Elder Erastus Snow, who served for
nearly 40 years as a member of the Council of Twelve,
and President Lorenzo Snow, who served for nearly
50 years in that Council and who then at the "young"
age of 84 commenced a three-year period as President of the Church.

I think I can pay no greater tribute to them than
to preach again a glorious doctrine which they taught
and which was one of the favorite themes, particularly of President Lorenzo Snow.

It has been said that one of his favorite passages
of scripture was the statement of the risen Lord to the
beloved John:

"To him that overcometh will I grant to sit with
me in my throne, even as I also overcame, and am
set down with my Father in his throne."

The teaching here involved is that men may be
perfect even as their Father in heaven is perfect. It
is that the Father is a glorified, exalted, and perfected
man who has all power, all might, and all dominion.

It is that Christ our Exemplar "received a fullness
of the glory of the Father," and that we too may advance and progress until we become like them and
have exaltation with them in the celestial kingdom.
We have been promised by the Lord that if we know
how to worship and know what we worship, we
may come unto the Father in his name and in due
time receive of his fullness. We have the promise
that if we keep his commandments, we shall receive
of his fullness and be glorified in him as he is in the
Father.

This is a doctrine that delighted President Snow,
as it does all of us. Early in his ministry, he received
by direct, personal revelation the knowledge that (in
the Prophet Joseph Smith's language) "God himself

was once as we are now, and is an exalted man, and sits enthroned in yonder heavens," and that men "have got to learn how to be Gods . . . the same as all Gods have done before."

After this doctrine had been taught by the Prophet, President Snow felt free to teach it also, and he summarized it in one of the best-known couplets in the Church in these words:

"As man now is, God once was;
As God now is, man may be."

This same doctrine has, of course, been known to the prophets of all the ages, and President Snow wrote an excellent poetic summary of it, which came to him as a result of pondering what some of the ancient prophets had written on the subject.

Now, I hold this glorious hope out to you as the goal toward which all members of the Church should strive. Our whole purpose in life should be to do those things which will enable us to gain eternal life, and eternal life is the kind of life possessed by the Father and the Son; it is exaltation in the eternal realms.

I remind you that eternal life is reserved for those who believe and obey, for those who keep the commandments, for those who enter into the Lord's law of eternal marriage and who then keep the covenant made incident to that holy order of matrimony.

24

*"The higher ordinances of
the priesthood and of
the gospel are reserved
to be performed in temples."*

Full Blessings of the Gospel

The cornerstone of the Provo, Utah, Temple—a white marble stone with gold-leaf lettering and containing a copper box filled with items of historical significance—was formally laid in ceremonies at the temple site May 21, 1971.

President Smith, who explained the purpose of temples to some 6,000 persons gathered for the impressive outdoor rites, was keynote speaker and presided at the ceremony, the second temple cornerstone ceremony over which he has presided since becoming President of the Church. The first was in Ogden, Utah, in September, 1970.

Twenty-two General Authorities, including all three members of the First Presidency, were in attendance at the Provo ceremony. Groundbreaking for the temple was held September 16, 1969, and its completion was set for the fall of 1971. The magnificent white-cast stone structure, located in northeast Provo, serves 33 stakes in eight regions in central Utah.

It is a glorious thing to build another house of the Lord, a house in which we can be taught the mysteries of the kingdom and in which the crowning ordinances of the gospel can be performed.

It is difficult to overstate the importance of temple building and of temple work. The Prophet Joseph Smith said one of the chief reasons for the very gathering of Israel is to enable the Saints to gain the blessings in these holy houses. And so it is that we, as a people, contribute of our means, make our time available, and use our talents and abilities in building temples so that the full blessings of the gospel may be made available for both the living and the dead.

May I now say just a few words about the purpose of temples. As you know, the Lord has commanded us to build temples, and the fact that we respond and go forward in this labor of love is one of the great evidences of the divinity of this work in which we are engaged.

We have received anew the fullness of the everlasting gospel. The Lord has given us every power, every key, every truth, and every ordinance necessary to gain salvation and exaltation in his kingdom. The fullness of the gospel consists of the fullness of these truths, powers, and ordinances needed to enable men to gain the fullness of reward in the celestial kingdom.

The higher ordinances of the priesthood and of the gospel are reserved to be performed in temples. The fullness of the priesthood is gained only in the temples, meaning there is no other place where the fullness of the blessings of the priesthood, of the Church, and of the gospel can be gained.

The fullness of the blessings of the priesthood and of the gospel grows out of celestial marriage. This is the crowning ordinance of the gospel, the crowning ordinance of the temple. It is through this order of matrimony that we are able to gain eternal life, to create for ourselves eternal family units of our own according to the plan of our Eternal Father.

There is nothing that ever comes into the life of a Latter-day Saint as important as entering into the proper temple marriage and of keeping the covenants made incident to that holy order of matrimony. Thus, we build temples for the benefit and blessing of the living, so that all of us may enter into those ordinances which lead to eternal life.

But in his infinite wisdom, the Lord has extended his arm of mercy to the dead as well as to the living. Through vicarious ordinances, it is our privilege to offer to our dead ancestors all of the blessings which have come to us.

Now, I pray that we shall use this temple to the fullest extent as soon as its facilities are available. There is no greater work than the work of the Lord, and there is nothing in this work more important to us as individuals than to receive the blessings of the house of the Lord and then so to live as to keep these eternal covenants in force so they will be binding on earth and sealed everlastingly in the heavens.

25

*"The fact that the Church is guided
by prophets—that it is presided
over by living oracles who
receive the mind and will of
the Lord—is conclusive proof
that it is the true church."*

"Hi, President Smith"

All morning, on May 28, 1971, the three girls waited
by the highway at Summit in southern Utah for President Smith's limousine to pass. They had heard that he
was to speak at Southern Utah State College in Cedar
City, and they wanted to get just a glimpse of him as he
passed.

Each girl held a sign, and the three signs together
read "Hi, President Smith." Hours later, as the President's
car passed, they were still standing by the road. However,
the reception they received from him far exceeded their
most-desired expectations. When President Smith saw
the girls, he had the car stopped and backed up, and he
shook their hands. He even asked to have the signs
they were holding. Later he received in the mail each of
the signs, with each girl's picture and biography on the
back.

At the college, President Smith addressed a forum,
sponsored by the Institute of Religion on campus. He
spoke on spiritual guidance.

I shall say a few words relative to living prophets
and the obligations we all have because we live in
the day when the Lord has his living oracles again
on earth.

89

We are all blessed far more than we realize because of our birth in a day when the gospel has
been restored and when the Church and kingdom of
God has again been established among men.

All my life, from my youngest days, I have felt
to thank the Lord that he has called prophets in this
day to lead and guide his people in paths of truth
and righteousness and to warn the world of the calamities that will befall them unless they repent and accept the gospel.

I was born when President Brigham Young was
still alive, and from the days of my youth to the
present time have had the privilege of sitting at the
feet of the prophets, of hearing their testimonies of
the divinity of this great work, and of feeling the
good spirit that comes from those who are in tune
with the Holy Ghost and who receive guidance from
the Lord.

The great men who have presided over this church
in past days and who have directed its affairs as
they in turn were guided by the Lord have truly
been the servants of the Most High. I rejoice in
walking in their footsteps and in following the course
they have charted.

May I say that the fact that the Church is guided
by prophets—that it is presided over by living oracles
who receive the mind and will of the Lord—is conclusive proof that it is the true church.

Now, I think that above all else in the world I,
and you, and all members of the Church should seek
to be guided by the Spirit of the Lord. To the extent
that we gain the guidance of that Spirit we will be
in harmony with those prophets whom the Lord has
placed in the First Presidency and in the Council of
the Twelve to guide and direct the affairs of his kingdom on earth.

However much we believe in education and want

all our young people to get all the schooling and training that in wisdom they can, we know that it is far more important for them so to live, and so to seek, that they may enjoy the companionship of the Holy Spirit.

Salvation comes by belief in the Lord and in his prophets. It comes to those who gain the companionship of the Spirit. It comes to those who accept and follow the apostles and prophets whom the Lord sends. It comes to those who love the Lord and who keep his commandments.

President Smith is a busy leader, signing papers, directing the activities of the Church.

In an outdoor ceremony, broadcast live over radio in Missouri, President Smith
addresses hugh crowd at dedication rites of new visitors center at Independence.

26

*"As the years pass, people in
all nations, from one end of the
earth to the other, are
increasingly turning to
Joseph Smith and the gospel restored
through his instrumentality."*

Hallowed by Memories

On a historic site hallowed by memories of what has
transpired, and sacred because of what is yet to come,
President Smith was principal speaker May 31, 1971, at
the dedication of a beautiful, modern visitors center in
Independence, Missouri.

The center, erected on a portion of the original 63
acres dedicated in 1831 by Joseph Smith for a magnificent
temple, portrays the story of the restoration of the gospel,
with emphasis on the second coming of Christ.

Nearly 5,000 persons—some coming from as far away
as 600 miles and some arriving six hours before the 7:00
P.M. ceremony—attended the dedication, held outdoors
under skies that cracked with lightning and reverberated
with thunder.

Midway through President Smith's address, a clap of
thunder boomed, followed by a flash of lightning. President Smith humorously commented, "I hardly expected
to fight the devil at the same time."

Because of the part which Jackson County, Missouri,
has played and will yet play in the glorious work of
restoration in this dispensation, I desire to call at-

93

tention to two great truths: first, that Jesus Christ is the Son of God, and second, that Joseph Smith is a prophet. I mention the first, which is one of the greatest truths ever revealed to man, as a prelude to bearing testimony of the second.

May I say, as plainly and as forcefully as I can, that we believe in Jesus Christ. We accept him without reservation as the Son of God and the Savior of the world.

We believe that he came into the world to ransom men from the temporal and spiritual death brought into the world through the fall of Adam, and we have in our hearts unbounded gratitude that through the shedding of his blood all men are raised in immortality, while those who believe and obey his laws are raised also unto eternal life.

We believe that salvation was, and is, and is to come in and through the atoning blood of Christ, the Lord Omnipotent, and that there is no other name given under heaven whereby men can become inheritors of eternal glory in the kingdoms which are ahead.

And may I say also, as plainly and forcefully as I can, that Joseph Smith, Jr., the prophet and seer of these latter days, was called by the Lord Jesus Christ to usher in this final dispensation and to restore for the last time on earth the fullness of his everlasting gospel.

Joseph Smith is the revealer of the knowledge of Christ and of salvation to the world for this day and generation. To him the Lord said, "This generation shall have my word through you."

When Moroni came to Joseph Smith nearly 150 years ago, that resurrected personage told the young prophet that his name should be had for good and evil among all nations, kindreds, and tongues, or that it should be both good and evil spoken of among all people.

Fifteen years later, the Lord himself elaborated upon this promise by saying to the Prophet: "The ends of the earth shall inquire after thy name, and fools shall have thee in derision, and hell shall rage against thee; While the pure in heart, and the wise, and the noble, and the virtuous, shall seek counsel, and authority, and blessings constantly from under thy hand."

I, for one, want to be numbered forever among those who seek counsel and authority and blessings as they have come from this great prophet whom the Lord raised up to commence the restoration of all things in this final, glorious gospel dispensation.

And I am pleased to testify that as the years pass, people in all nations, from one end of the earth to the other, are increasingly turning to Joseph Smith and the gospel restored through his instrumentality in order to find peace in this life and gain a hope of eternal life in the world to come.

Joseph Smith is the one to whom all men must look in this day to learn the truth about Christ and his gospel. I revere and honor his holy name. And I, for one, want to be an instrument in the Lord's hands of letting the ends of the earth know that salvation is again available because the Lord raised up a mighty seer in this day to reestablish his kingdom on earth.

Hugh crowds gather around President Smith as he leaves fieldhouse at Brigham Young University.

27

*"Our eventual goal is to
gain all knowledge and all power
and be like our Eternal
Father and have exaltation ourselves."*

A Golden Era

Five thousand persons from 20 states, including Alaska and Hawaii, attended the opening general assembly June 8, 1971, of BYU Education Week in Provo, Utah, to listen to words of counsel from President Smith. On this occasion he stressed the value of education in the lives of Latter-day Saints.

The assembly marked the beginning of the fiftieth anniversary—the Golden Era—of BYU education weeks, originally called "leadership weeks." Eleven persons present at the assembly had participated in the first event in January, 1922.

Education weeks are now held at some 60 locations throughout the United States, Canada, and Mexico.

In this life, there are few things as important as proper education. As a church and as a people we have always been foremost in the warfare against ignorance and bigotry and lack of knowledge and understanding among men.

In the Church, we are not limited to the usual standards of judgment which are common in the world; but in addition, we have the spirit of inspiration from the Lord.

There is something unique about our system of education and training. We believe in intellectual pursuits and hope all our young people will gain that schooling which is best adapted to their individual talents and circumstances. But we believe in spiritual as well as intellectual education.

Our theme speaks of a golden era of continuing education, but this pursuit of education is only part of our over-all goal, which is to usher in a golden era of continuing righteousness.

I suppose there have only been two times in the entire history of the world when whole peoples have become so learned in the things of the Spirit that perfect eras of continuing righteousness have prevailed. Those times were in the days of Enoch and among the Nephites following our Lord's ministry on the American continent.

We are now living in the Saturday night of time, and the day will soon come when the Lord will usher in the great millennium, which will be a thousand years of peace and light and learning under perfect conditions.

But until that day arrives, we should prepare ourselves by seeking learning, even by study and also by faith.

The secular or worldly knowledge we gain will benefit us in our temporal pursuits, but the knowledge we gain of spiritual and eternal truths will prepare us to live everlastingly in the kingdom of our Eternal Father. In the Church School System, we strive to gain both secular and eternal education.

My counsel is that we should gain as much knowledge and wisdom as we can, "of things both in heaven and in the earth, and under the earth; things which have been, things which are, things which must shortly come to pass; things which are at home, things which are abroad; the wars and the perplexities of the nations, and the judgments which are on the land; and a knowledge also of countries and of kingdoms."

But more particularly, my counsel is that we should "be instructed more perfectly in theory, in principle, in doctrine, in the law of the gospel, in all things that pertain unto the kingdom of God."

The Prophet Joseph Smith taught that man is saved no faster than he gains knowledge of God and his laws, and that no man can be saved in ignorance of Jesus Christ and the truths of his everlasting gospel.

Knowledge comes both by reason and by revelation. We are expected to study and learn all we can by research and analysis. But there are limits to our learning abilities in the realms of reason and study. The things of God can be known only by the Spirit of God. We must gain knowledge by faith.

As the Prophet wrote in Liberty Jail: "God shall give unto you knowledge by his Holy Spirit, yea, the unspeakable gift of the Holy Ghost."

If we are faithful in all things, our eventual goal is to gain all knowledge and all power and be like our Eternal Father and have exaltation ourselves.

My grandfather, the Patriarch Hyrum Smith, said at the last general conference of the Church before his martyrdom, "I would not serve a God that had not all wisdom and all power."

Christ is the great prototype of salvation. Of him, the revelation says: "He received a fulness of truth, yea, even of all truth; And no man receiveth a fulness unless he keepeth his commandments. He that keepeth his commandments receiveth truth and light, until he is glorified in truth and knoweth all things."

28

"Each one of you has been called by the spirit of prophecy; you have been called by inspiration."

The Work of Saving Souls

The 1971 mission presidents' seminar was held June 21-23, 1971, in Salt Lake City. Twenty-nine presidents and their wives, called to serve in various mission fields throughout· the world, heard counsel and instruction during the three-day seminar.

President Smith spoke to them on June 22 on the importance of their callings; other General Authorities and officers of the Church instructed them on the various Church programs.

You are a very choice group who have been carefully selected for the great work that lies ahead. There is nothing any of you could do for the time and season of this appointment that would be as important as it is.

As all of us know, the Lord has restored his everlasting gospel in these last days for the salvation of his children here on earth. This gospel—which we have received and which we are commanded to offer to all men everywhere—is the plan of salvation, and all who will believe and obey its laws shall be saved in the kingdom of God.

Thus, we are engaged in the most important and glorious work in the world—the work of saving souls. And the Lord's hand is in this work. He is guiding the Church; he is directing its destiny; and he is opening up the way for the spread of truth in the nations of the earth in a marvelous manner.

Now, may I say that each one of you has been called by the spirit of prophecy; you have been called by inspiration; the Lord's hand has been manifest in your selection to fill the positions assigned to you. You may all go forth with this assurance.

And may I say also that the words which the Lord spoke to John Whitmer and to others in the beginning days of this dispensation apply equally to you. They are: "And now, behold, I say unto you, that the thing which will be of the most worth unto you will be to declare repentance unto this people, that you may bring souls unto me, that you may rest with them in the kingdom of my Father."

May I remind those of you who have sacrificed your personal interests to go forth to the various nations to preach the gospel of the reward that will be yours if you are faithful in all things.

The wage that the Lord of the harvest pays to the laborers in his vineyard is eternal life in his kingdom.

It will now be your privilege to devote your full time and all your strength and energies in the Lord's work. You will associate with and preside over some of the choicest young people who have ever lived on earth; they are spirits who were kept in reserve to come forth in this latter dispensation to take the message of salvation to the nations of the earth, and I am sure all of you will rejoice in your association and labors with them. Your first and chief responsibility will be the spiritual and temporal well-being of your missionaries.

President Smith, who directs the activities of a three-million member worldwide church, ponders a matter in the council room in the Church Office Building.

Now, please be assured that you are going forth on the Lord's errand with the blessings and prayers of the First Presidency and of the Council of the Twelve and of all the Brethren. The parents of thousands of missionaries and countless other members of the Church will be praying for your well-being and that you will have the inspiration to guide and enlighten your fellow missionaries.

You are going forth to succeed and not to fail. The Lord's work does not fail. You are going forth to find peace and joy in your ministries here and to lay up treasures in heaven that will multiply in due course to eternal life there.

President Smith visits with new Arizona Temple president, C. Bryant Whiting, left, and released president, Jesse M. Smith, in Mesa, Arizona.

29

"There is no work connected
with the gospel that is of a
more unselfish nature
than the work in the house of
the Lord for our dead."

Temple Reorganizations

During the first year of President Smith's administration, he called and set apart new presidencies of four temples in Utah, Idaho, Arizona, and California. At each of these reorganizations, he met with temple workers and explained the "unselfish nature of the work" in which they were engaged. He also paid tribute to the outgoing presidencies and introduced the new temple presidents.

The first reorganization was at Los Angeles Temple on March 8, 1970, followed by the Arizona Temple at Mesa on August 31, 1970; the Idaho Falls Temple on October 20, 1970; and the St. George Temple on November 8, 1970.

May I say this to you about the unselfish nature of the work in which you are engaged: There is no work connected with the gospel that is of a more unselfish nature than the work in the house of the Lord for our dead. Those who work for the dead do not expect to receive any earthly remuneration or reward. It is, above all, a work of love that is begotten in the heart of man through faithful and constant labor in these saving ordinances. There are no financial returns, but there shall be great joy in heaven with those souls whom we have helped to their salvation.

It is a work that enlarges the soul of man, broadens his views regarding the welfare of his fellowman, and plants in his heart a love for all the children of our Heavenly Father. There is no work equal to that in the temple for the dead in teaching a man to love his neighbor as himself.

Jesus so loved the world that he was willing to offer himself as a sacrifice for sin that the world might be saved. We also have the privilege, in a small degree, of showing our great love for him and our fellow beings by helping them to receive the blessings of the gospel that now they cannot receive without our assistance.

We should consider the Latter-day Saints the most blessed people of all times: blessed with the knowledge of salvation for the human family both living and dead.

For hundreds of years the world was in spiritual darkness. The Lord came and brought light and truth to be a benefit to all mankind if they would repent and receive the sacred blessing of the Lord Jesus Christ. The Twelve of that dispensation went forth and did all in their power to teach a fallen world. They once had the idea that the gospel was only for the children of Israel. The Lord corrected that. The gospel is something that pertains to every human soul born into this world.

That is why today we build temples. That is why men and women are spending their time and talent in the temples of the Lord and are endeavoring to teach a dissatisfied humanity the plan of salvation by which they can come back again into the presence of the Son of God.

We are living in the dispensation of the fullness of times, the last dispensation before the coming of the Son of God. The work before us as members of the Church is extensive; we have the privilege of doing the labor for those who do not have the opportunity to do the work. We take to them salvation on the condition of repentance.

We have today many temples; we are going to have more in which we may have the privilege of going and giving to the dead the opportunity of salvation.

Let us live the gospel the way we know we should so that the Lord will continue to bless and prosper us. If this is our course, we shall truly be instruments in his hands of bringing to pass much righteousness.

30

"When we are baptized,
we covenant to walk
in virtue and holiness
before the Lord."

The Lord's Work

During the first part of 1971, President Smith addressed four stake conferences in the Salt Lake area, stressing the covenants members make with the Lord at the time of baptism and marriage. He spoke to Wells Stake conference March 7; Riverside Stake conference, March 21; Valley View Stake conference, May 2; and Grant Stake conference, June 20.

It is not position or prominence in the Church that qualifies us for the blessings of the gospel, but our obedience to the commandments of the Lord. When we are baptized, we covenant to walk in virtue and holiness before the Lord; to contribute of our time and means for the building up of the Church; and to serve our fellowmen with an eye single to the glory of God. The Lord on his part promises to pour out his Spirit more abundantly upon us and to give us eternal life in his kingdom.

When we are married in the temple, we covenant to keep all the terms and conditions of the new and everlasting covenant of marriage; to be true to our companions; to multiply and replenish the earth; and to bring up our children in light and truth. The Lord on his part promises that the family unit shall endure forever and that all its faithful members shall have eternal life.

These great gospel blessings are available for all of us. I pray that we may come to an understanding of the laws of the Lord and live in harmony with them, that we may keep our covenants and gain all of the rich blessings promised the saints. This is the Lord's work in which we are engaged, and it is true.

31

President and Sister Smith
were always together. They enjoyed
being alone in their
apartment. When he traveled, she
was by his side. When she was
ill, he was at her side.

Tribute to Jessie Evans Smith

Every day began and ended with a kiss for President and Sister Joseph Fielding Smith, who celebrated their thirty-third wedding anniversary on April 12, 1971.

"Now, Joseph, kiss your wife," was the expression used by President Heber J. Grant after he had performed the early morning ceremony in the Salt Lake Temple in 1938. "He said it like he meant it, and I have been doing it ever since," President Smith said.

"It couldn't be nicer," Sister Smith added. "There's never been a cross word." To this President Smith replied, "I don't know any cross words. I can't use them if I don't know them."

The importance of family togetherness and understanding is well known to President Smith. His wife was his constant companion and helpmate, buoying him up in his travels and responsibilities as President of the Church.

"Sister Smith is very helpful to me," President Smith said on one occasion. "She is such a happy, pleasant person. We enjoy each other and often spend time studying together. The wives of the Church leaders should be happy, helpful wives," he said.

President and Sister Smith were noted for their duets. Wherever they traveled, as the opportunity presented itself, they would sing together.

Sister Smith, as she concluded her remarks, would sometimes say in whispered but forceful tones, "I think I can persuade the President to sing a duet with me. Would you like to hear it?"

The reaction was always enthusiastic; often the audiences would respond by clapping.

"They want us," she would say, starting for the piano and at the same time giving the signal to President Smith.

Walking slowly to the microphone, he would say in a little bit of a gruff voice, "This isn't a duet—it's a do-it." Then, with a smile, he would take his wife by the arm and they would go to the piano.

Seated side by side, with Sister Smith playing the piano, they would sing, "If I Knew You and You Knew Me."

The crowds loved it.

President Smith carried with him a keen wit and Sister Smith carried with her a bag of tricks and jokes.

"Have you seen my Texas note pad?" she would say, taking from her handbag a leather-covered pad filled with dollar bills.

They enjoyed riding in their automobile, usually a compact car and often with Sister Smith at the wheel. It was an opportunity to relax; it was an opportunity to be with each other. They didn't go far, just around the familiar areas that were important and beautiful to them.

They did their shopping together, using care to buy only at stores that were closed on Sundays. They liked to go to plays and other entertainment.

President Smith often accompanied his wife on shopping trips. They always shopped at stores that closed their doors on Sunday.

President Smith's birthday celebrations in the park were attended by all the family, but "our wedding anniversary we celebrate together," Sister Smith said.

"Do you remember, Daddy dear, the one thing that sticks in our minds more than anything else is what President Grant said to us when we were married. He said, 'You are married for time and for all eternity. Not just time and eternity, but time and all eternity.' "

President and Sister Smith were always together. They enjoyed being alone in their apartment, shelves filled with books, mementos placed about the room, and a grand piano. When he traveled, she was by his side. When she was ill, he was at her side. The last weeks of her illness, he stayed at the hospital to be near her. On August 3, 1971, when she died, he was at her side. An earthly life of beautiful companionship came to a close.

Sister Smith was honored by BYU First Stake at a ten-stake fireside attended by 14,200 students.

32

"The chief business of our lives is to build a house that will bear the weight of eternal life."

The Diamond
(An address by Sister Smith)

Sister Jessie Evans Smith, who died in Salt Lake City August 3, 1971, received a great honor November 1, 1970, when she was honored by 14,200 Brigham Young University students in Provo, Utah.

Sister Smith was invited by the BYU First Stake to speak at a ten-stake fireside in George Albert Smith Fieldhouse. The congregation was the largest audience ever to pay tribute to President and Sister Smith since President Smith assumed the leadership of the Church in January, 1970. About 12,500 students filled the fieldhouse; another 1,700 were in two other buildings, where the fireside was carried by closed-circuit broadcast.

President and Sister Smith were visibly touched by the huge, receptive congregation, who stood and sang "We Thank Thee, O God, for a Prophet" as the Smiths entered the fieldhouse. After the fireside was over, all stood and sang the song again, this time all three verses, giving thanks in music for the experience they just had of sharing an hour with President Smith and his wife.

The demand for personal purity is made by the Church upon both men and women equally. There is no double standard of judgment. I am sure that if we follow the ways of the Lord, our pathways will lead us to do the right thing.

One of the greatest responsibilities that is ever
entrusted to any human being is that of building his
own personality. The chief business of our lives is
to build a house that will bear the weight of eternal
life. God has instructed us to use only the finest
materials.

He cannot look upon sin with the least degree of
allowance, because he knows its terrible destructive-
ness in peoples' lives. God has provided that every
man should carry within himself the very things that
he seeks: faith, courage, and love. And we can develop that with which we have already been endowed. We should develop the ability to do the right
things instead of allowing ourselves endlessly to do
as we please.

From the beginning of time, the five most precious of all gems have been rubies, sapphires, emeralds, pearls, and diamonds. These have been the
most frequently used in the crowns of royalty. There
is an old song that says, "Shall I have many stars
in my crown?" Now, I know that we will each have
as many stars as we deserve, and they will be of our
own choosing. We will also have an ornament of
crowns of most precious jewels. In speaking to Mal-
achi, the Lord talks about the day when he will
make up his jewels. You are all given that important
privilege and responsibility, and inasmuch as we
may make our own selections, what jewels should
we choose?

The ruby is the symbol of courage and valor. It
is thought by some to be more valuable than diamonds. In making up our jewels we should have a
good supply of gems of courage. Think how our lives
sparkle with a few precious blood-red rubies in our
crown.

Second, our crown jewels should include sapphires. The sapphire is the gem of truth, sincerity,

and loyalty. Some of the ancient peoples believed that the earth rested upon a giant sapphire, which gave the sky a blue color. The sapphire has been called the celestial stone. What could make one more kingly in his life or more loved of the Lord than to have in his crown the diadem of truth and to hold in his hand the scepter of righteousness?

The third of our precious gems is the emerald, the jewel of friendship. The life of Deity himself might very fittingly be represented by the emerald, "For God so loved the world . . . that whosoever believeth in him should not perish, but have everlasting life." When we make up our jewels we should include a generous supply of emeralds.

The fourth gem is the pearl. The pearl is the symbol of wisdom, the jewel of purity and modesty. Jesus used the term *the pearl of great price* to indicate the most important of all values.

Then we come to the last of the precious stones; the diamond is the king of gems. It is the hardest substance known. Nothing can cut a diamond except another diamond. The diamond is the gem of constancy and skill. It stands for industry and utility. It is prized for its hardness, its clear beauty, and its unusual ability to flash beautiful colors when light strikes it. No crown would be complete without the symbolism, beauty, and utility of some brilliant diamond.

While some of us may never wear a real crown, each of us wears a crown just the same. Each will determine the number of stars of accomplishment that it contains and the kind of jewels by which it will be adorned. Certainly the great character qualities symbolized by the precious gems are far more valuable than the jewels in the tower of London. The enemies of Jesus placed a crown of thorns upon his head, but God crowned him with eternal glory.

33

*"I honor and revere
the name and the memory of
President David O. McKay."*

A True Servant of the Lord

On January 18, 1970, President David O. McKay, 96,
ninth President of the Church, died in Salt Lake City after
a long illness. President McKay, who had served as a
General Authority longer than any other person, had been
President for nearly 19 years and was deeply involved in
an era of explosive progress for the Church.

His body lay in state for three days in the Church
Office Building. Tens of thousands of Church members
lined the sidewalks around the Church Administration
block, often in drizzling rain, waiting to file past the
body of the man who, in the minds of millions of people
throughout the world, was the epitome of goodness.

President Smith, a counselor to President McKay since
1965 and President of the Council of Twelve, was one of
the speakers at the funeral, held January 22, 1970, in
the Tabernacle on Temple Square.

The following day President Joseph Fielding Smith
was ordained , and set apart as the tenth President of
The Church of Jesus Christ of Latter-day Saints.

I honor and revere the name and the memory of
President David O. McKay. For 60 years, I sat by his
side in the presiding councils of the Church. I came
to know him intimately and well, and I loved him
as a man and honored him as a prophet.

He was a true servant of our Lord—one who
walked uprightly before his Maker; one who loved

his fellowmen; one who loved life and rejoiced in the privilege of service that was his; one who served with an eye single to the glory of God.

He exemplified perfectly the Old Testament standard: "what doth the Lord require of thee, but to do justly, and to love mercy, and to walk humbly with thy God?"

President McKay was called to the holy apostleship in April, 1906, by my father, President Joseph F. Smith, who acted under the inspiration of the Spirit, and he became one of the greatest and most inspired leaders of this dispensation.

In the early days of his ministry the Brethren used to go out on assignments two by two. Often President McKay and I went together. We would travel as far as we could by train and then the local brethren would meet us with a white top or a wagon. Sometimes we continued on horses or mules or by ox team. Many times we slept out under the stars or in such houses or cabins as were available.

In all his travels President McKay was a perfect gentleman—always kind and considerate, more interested in my comfort than in his own.

I shall miss him greatly. It does not seem possible that he has left us. But we know he has gone to a joyous reunion with his father and mother and that he is now taking up his labors in the paradise of God as he begins to associate anew with his good friends who preceded him into the realms ahead, with Stephen L Richards and J. Reuben Clark, with George Albert Smith and Heber J. Grant, with Henry D. Moyle and Joseph F. Smith, and a host of others.

I thank God for the life and ministry of this great man. He was a soul set apart, a great spirit who came here to preside in Israel. He did his work well and has returned clean and perfected to the realms of light and joyous reunion.

34

"Sister McKay was a woman of rare charm, of simple faith, and of sound judgment."

A Choice Spirit

Sister Emma Ray Riggs McKay, 93, widow of President David O. McKay, died in her Hotel Utah apartment in Salt Lake City, Utah, November 14, 1970, after a long period of failing health. Her death marked the end of an era in the Church. President McKay had preceded her in death on January 18, 1970, at the age of 96.

Four days later, funeral services for Sister McKay were held in the Assembly Hall on Temple Square, under the direction of the First Presidency. President Smith was one of the speakers at the funeral.

I deem it an honor to have this privilege of saying a few words at this service, and of paying tribute to Sister Emma Ray Riggs McKay, one of the great women of the Church and the wife and eternal companion of one of the greatest men of our day and age.

She was a choice spirit, one sent here to stand by his side, to bear his children, to be a comfort and a helpmeet to him. And she also did her work well and has returned as he did, clean and perfected, to the realms of light and joyous reunion.

Sister McKay was a woman of rare charm, of simple faith, and of sound judgment whose greatest achievements grew out of her role as a wife and a mother. President McKay said that no success can compensate for failure in the home, and Sister McKay rose to the challenge and with her husband set an example for the whole Church where the family and the truly basic and important things of life are concerned.

The family unit is the most important organization in time or eternity. President and Sister McKay have become the symbol of this perfect order of matrimony for the Church in this day. Their lives have been the perfect example of mutual consideration, love, and respect.

Great and important as was their service in the Church and in the world, their greatest blessings have and shall come out of the eternal family unit.

I have no hesitancy in saying that after the separation of the ten months since President McKay's passing, they have now been reunited in the paradise of God, and that they shall rise together in due course in the morning of the first resurrection to inherit the fullness of our Father's blessings.

In the language of the revelation on marriage: "They shall pass by the angels, and the gods, which are set there, to their exaltation and glory in all things, as hath been sealed upon their heads, which glory shall be a fulness and a continuation of the seeds forever and ever."

35

"To the faithful members of
the Church, death is not
something to be feared.
It is simply the final, necessary
experience of mortality."

A Message of Comfort

A message of peace and comfort to those whose lives
have been struck by physical ailments and death was
given November 11, 1970, by President Smith as he spoke
at the funeral services in the Salt Lake Tabernacle for
Elder Thrope B. Isaacson, Assistant to the Council of the
Twelve, who had served in the First Presidency with
President Smith under the late President David O. McKay.

Elder Isaacson, 72, suffered a stroke in February, 1966,
and had been ill from then until his death on November
9, 1970.

Elder Isaacson was true to the faith, valiant in the
cause of righteousness, and devoted to those principles
by which men gain peace and joy in this life and
prepare themselves for the glories of the life to
come. As a church and as a people we are glad he
served his mortal probation in our day and that we
have been blessed because of the great talents and
abilities with which he was so abundantly endowed.

During the latter years of his life, Brother Isaacson

was subject to the ills of the flesh and suffered a great deal because he was unable to carry on in that forceful and energetic way to which he was accustomed. Now a merciful and gracious Father has called him to continue his labors in another sphere where he is free from disease and afflictions and where he can preach the gospel and serve on the Lord's errand without any restrictions or hindrance.

To the faithful members of the Church, death is not something to be feared. It is simply the final, necessary experience of mortality; and it consists of the transfer of the righteous soul to another sphere, a sphere where the Lord's work still rolls on and where joy and peace reign.

To Brother Isaacson's family, and to all those who are left by the Lord to suffer serious physical ailments, I desire to say that even good and righteous people are sanctified by suffering. We are here in mortality to gain experiences that we could not gain in any other way. The Son of God himself, while he dwelt in the flesh, was called upon to "suffer temptations, and pain of body, hunger, thirst, and fatigue, even more than man can suffer, except it be unto death."

Some of us receive our trials in one way and some in another, but it is an eternal principle that, as Paul said, "Whom the Lord loveth, he chasteneth, and scourgeth every son whom he receiveth." And those saints who endure valiantly and who bear with patience the burdens placed upon them in this life shall rise to glory and honor in the life to come.

Here we are mortal; there we shall be immortal. Here we gain experience through suffering; there we shall have physical perfection and no longer be in bondage to disease and sorrow and mortal handicaps.

If a man came into this life and was never tempted and tried, he would miss something. Resisting evil

President Smith is a familiar figure at the pulpit in the Salt Lake Tabernacle.

helps to make us strong, physically and morally, and beyond that, spiritually. The Lord has never left his children unattended to the buffetings of Satan. We have access to our Father through our prayers. We have the gospel.

We came to be tried and tested to see if we could return to our Father in heaven. We came here to suffer pain and affliction. This is part of our mortal probation that we may come back into his presence and that glory of the fullness that is promised us.

President Joseph Fielding Smith enjoys walking and meeting people. At Alderly Edge in England, he asks some young people about their dog.

36

*"We are and shall be a
world church. That is
our destiny. It is
part of the Lord's program."*

A Worldwide Church

The first area general conference of the Church, designed to bring leadership and various programs closer to its members, was held August 27-29, 1971, in Manchester, England. President Smith and 13 other General Authorities and five auxiliary leaders participated in the conference, attended by thousands of Saints of Great Britain from nine stakes and seven missions.

President Smith gave five speeches during the three-day conference, held in King's Hall in Bell Vue Park and in nearby Free Trade Hall. He spoke at an adult leadership meeting and a youth session on August 27; the opening general session and priesthood meeting on August 28, and the closing session on August 29.

President Joseph Fielding Smith enjoyed his visit to England. It brought back memories of his missionary days served in Nottingham. Following the conference President Smith was driven by automobile to the area of his missionary service.

"I lived in the upstairs room of a widow's home. It was three stories up, I think, and on a very narrow street. On the other side of that street was a garment factory and it was running night and day. It made such an awful racket that we could hardly sleep at night," he recalled.

"We spoke at a number of places on street corners and went from door to door, always walking. It seemed that we never rode a foot," he said.

During his stay in England, President Smith enjoyed
several rides in the country. At Alderly Edge he took a
long walk down a foot path to the edge of a cliff overlooking the country side. He paused on the way to talk
with children and posed with them for a picture.

England holds a special spot in the heart of President
Smith.

Adult Leadership Session

You are the most choice and blessed and favored
people in this entire nation because you belong to
The Church of Jesus Christ of Latter-day Saints; because you have taken upon you the name of Christ,
with a covenant to love and serve him all your days;
and because you are on the path leading to eternal
life in our Father's kingdom.

It is a matter of great satisfaction to me and my
Brethren that the Church has now grown to the point
that it seems wise and necessary to hold general conferences in various nations. And what could be more
appropriate than to begin this new advancement here
in the British Isles, the place from which so much of
the strength of the Church came, in the early days of
this dispensation.

I suppose all of you know that all of the Presidents
of the Church except the Prophet Joseph Smith have
performed missionary service in this great nation. I
served as a young missionary here over seventy years
ago, and many great things have transpired in the
Church and in the world since that day, not the least
of which is the holding of this conference.

We are members of a world church, a church that
has the plan of life and salvation, a church set up by
the Lord himself in these last days to carry his message of salvation to all his children in all the earth.

The day is long since past when informed people
think of us as a peculiar group in the tops of the
Rocky Mountains in America. It is true that the

Church headquarters are in Salt Lake City and that the Lord's house has been erected there to which people have come from many nations to learn the law of the Lord and to walk in his paths.

But now we are coming of age as a church and as a people. We have attained the stature and strength that are enabling us to fulfill the commission given us by the Lord through the Prophet Joseph Smith, that we should carry the glad tidings of the restoration to every nation and to all people.

And not only shall we preach the gospel in every nation before the second coming of the Son of Man, but we shall make converts and establish congregations of Saints among them. We are and shall be a world church. This is our destiny. It is part of the Lord's program.

"The covenant people of the Lord" are "scattered upon all the face of the earth," and it is our commission to go into all nations and gather these elect into the Church and to bring them to a knowledge of their Redeemer, so they shall be heirs of salvation in his kingdom. Thus, the Church is not an American church. It is not a Canadian church; it is not an Australian church; it is not a British church. The Church of Jesus Christ is a world church, and the gospel is for all men.

The gospel itself is the same in every nation. There is only one plan of salvation. There is only one way for men to gain a celestial inheritance of eternal glory, and that is to forsake the world, have faith in the Lord Jesus Christ, enter his kingdom through the door of baptism, receive the gift of the Holy Ghost, and then keep his commandments.

Now, may I say that as the members of the kingdom come to a knowledge of the worldwide stature of the Church, they will see that this imposes added responsibilities upon the Saints in each nation.

Joseph Smith was asked how he governed so great and diverse a people as the Latter-day Saints. He replied: "I teach them correct principles and they govern themselves."

This is the principle upon which we operate in the Church. We expect our members everywhere to learn correct principles and to govern themselves. We desire to see the Saints in every nation receive the full blessings of the gospel and stand as spiritual leaders in their nations.

The Saints in Great Britain are entitled to every blessing and spiritual gift as rapidly as they can qualify themselves to receive them. The Lord never withholds any good thing from his faithful Saints if they are prepared to receive it.

We want the Church to grow and flourish here. You already have a temple dedicated to the Lord in which you can receive those ordinances and blessings out of which exaltation grows. We hope to see the day when there will be stakes of Zion in every part of the land, and the people of Great Britain must qualify themselves for service in the wards and stakes. The missionary work among the millions of our Father's children who dwell in this favored part of the earth should be done in large measure by your own people.

We can see a great future for the Church here and hope all the British Saints will do their duty and qualify to further the work of the kingdom and do all they must to work out their salvation. The greatest need of the Saints in all nations is to keep the commandments and so live as to have the companionship of the Holy Spirit. Through such a course, the Saints of all nations shall truly be one, the Lord will be pleased with our labors, and the work will prosper everywhere.

Members of the First Presidency enjoy pause in conference session in the
Tabernacle.

President Joseph Fielding Smith, at 95 years of age, thrills capacity audience at King's Hall during area general conference in England.

37

*"The destiny of the
Church rests with the
youth of Zion."*

Future Leaders of the Church

Thousands of young men and women crowded the hall in Manchester, England, to see the Prophet and hear his testimony. They had looked forward with anxiety to being in the presence of President Joseph Fielding Smith. They were not disappointed, for he left the adult session of the conference following his opening address to meet with the young people of Britain.

Recorded messages had been played of former presidents of the Church, including Presidents Wilford Woodruff, Joseph F. Smith, Heber J. Grant, George Albert Smith, and David O. McKay. Now, standing before them was a living prophet. The feeling was awesome as President Smith spoke. He talked their language, he had a message for the youth, and they heard him say, "I know . . ."

Youth Session

As you know, the Lord has revealed his eternal plan of salvation in a number of gospel dispensations. We live in the greatest of these, the dispensation of the fulness of times which was ushered in by the personal appearance of the Father and the Son in the spring of 1820 to Joseph Smith, who was then in his fifteenth year.

133

The gospel itself has been the same in all dispensations; the plan of salvation is the same for all our Father's children in every age. From time to time it has been lost by apostasy, but whenever the Lord has had a people on earth, they have been offered the same laws and truths of salvation that he has revealed to us.

But there is one great added thing that we have received in this age that has never been had before. In this dispensation, the Lord has decreed that the Church shall never again be led astray; this time the gospel is here to stay. This time the revealed truth is destined to prepare a people for the second coming of the Son of Man, and the Church will be established in all parts of the earth when the Lord comes to usher in the millennial era of peace and righteousness.

Now, I say these things to you to make it clear that the destiny of the Church rests with the youth of Zion. The Church is here to stay, and the young and rising generation shall rise up and direct the kingdom in due course with great power and glory. It is true that some of our youth may be led astray and fall into forbidden paths. But the generality of them will remain faithful.

One thing this means is that among you are the future bishops and stake presidents, the future mission presidents and temple presidents here in Great Britain. You are the future leaders, and because of the great work that lies ahead for you, you have a special obligation to stand true and steadfast to the standards of the Church. Satan will tempt you, but if you will remain true to every trust, the Lord will guide and enlighten and preserve you for the labors ahead.

I hope that all the worthy and qualified young men among you may have the privilege of missionary service. There is a great need for more missionary service from among the youth of the Church here. We need to send our young missionaries from America, and some of you also, for that matter, to some of the populous nations of the earth that have scarcely been touched as yet with the preaching of the gospel. The youth of Great Britain need to qualify to do the missionary work here and to help in other areas.

The crowning goal in your life should be to go to the house of the Lord and be sealed for eternity to a choice companion. It is out of this relationship that the greatest joys and satisfactions of both time and eternity shall come to you.

I want you to know that I know that we are engaged in the Lord's work. I want you to know that this work is true. I know that The Church of Jesus Christ of Latter-day Saints is the kingdom of God on earth and that the gospel is destined to roll forward until it fills the whole earth.

President Harold B. Lee, first counselor in the First Presidency, confers with
President Smith during the all-British area conference in Manchester, England.

38

*"We do not look back
to the Bible alone for
our knowledge of the
Lord and his laws."*

The Plan of Salvation

The love of the British members of the Church was manifested immediately when President Joseph Fielding Smith entered King's Hall for the opening of the first area general conference held in Great Britain.

"We should sing 'We Thank Thee, O God for a Prophet,'" one lady said as he entered.

The audience stood in respectful quiet.

"The Prophet passed within 20 feet of where I was standing," a man said, overjoyed at being so near the President of the Church.

When he was congratulated on his opening address to the conference, he softly said, "I didn't come here to fail."

And fail he did not. The people manifested their love with hallowed respect. They rejoiced at seeing him.

But if their love was apparent for him, it did not exceed his love for them.

Opening General Session

We have received the fullness of the everlasting gospel; that is, the Lord has revealed to us his plan of salvation and given us the power and authority to preach the gospel, to perform the ordinances of salvation, and to do all the things which will enable us to gain the fullness of reward in his kingdom.

Let us make this very plain: We do not look back to the Bible alone for our knowledge of the Lord and his laws. We do not claim priesthood or power or authority from heaven because these were possessed by the ancient saints. Our roots are not buried in the rubble of past ages.

It is true that we believe the Bible more literally and fully and completely, I am sure, than others do. We accept it as "the word of God," and strive to live in harmony with its teachings. We have all the knowledge that the world has about the dealings of the Lord with people in former times. But the gospel which we have received has come to us by revelation, by the opening of the heavens, by the ministering of angels in modern times.

This church administers the gospel and makes salvation available to all who will believe and obey those eternal laws which Deity has ordained to prepare men for life in his presence. We believe that salvation is in Christ, that he is the Savior of the world and the Redeemer of men.

We accept without reservation the scriptural teachings that Christ is the Son of God and that he came into the world to ransom men from the spiritual and temporal death brought into the world by the fall of Adam. No one can state too plainly or emphasize too strongly this eternal truth that salvation is in Christ and that it comes because of his atoning sacrifice.

Because of his atoning sacrifice, all men will be raised in immortality. They will come forth from the grave and live forever as resurrected beings. But only those who believe and obey the fullness of his laws shall be raised both in immortality and unto eternal life. And one of the great purposes of the true church is to teach men what they must do after baptism to gain the full blessings of the gospel.

Building on the foundation of the atonement, the plan of salvation consists of the following things:

First, we must have faith in the Lord Jesus Christ; we must accept him as the Son of God; we must put our trust in him, rely upon his word, and desire to gain the blessings which come by obedience to his laws.

Second, we must repent of our sins; we must forsake the world; we must determine in our hearts, without reservation, that we will live godly and upright lives.

Third, we must be baptized in water, under the hands of a legal administrator who has power to bind on earth and seal in heaven; we must through this sacred ordinance enter into a covenant to serve the Lord and keep his commandments.

Fourth, we must receive the gift of the Holy Ghost; we must be born again; we must have sin and iniquity burned out of our souls as though by fire; we must gain a new creation by the power of the Holy Ghost.

Fifth, we must endure to the end; we must keep the commandments after baptism; we must work out our salvation with fear and trembling before the Lord; we must so live as to acquire the attributes of godliness and become the kind of people who can enjoy the glory and wonders of the celestial kingdom.

President Joseph Fielding Smith addresses the largest priesthood meeting ever held to date in Great Britain during the area general conference. Nearly 2,000 men and boys heard the President tell of the importance of the priesthood.

39

*"We are to use the
priesthood to bless
ourselves and to
bless mankind."*

The Authority of God

The largest priesthood meeting ever held in Great
Britain met in Free Trade Hall at Manchester, England, on
August 28, 1971. The men and boys in attendance numbered 1,954. They represented the priesthood in England,
Scotland, Ireland, and Wales. President Smith had prepared some short opening remarks, but when he was introduced to the vast audience of priesthood brethren by
President Harold B. Lee, he was so impressed and inspired
that he spoke from his heart for 25 minutes.

No young man, no father in attendance at that meeting will ever forget hearing the Prophet of the Lord say,
"The priesthood is the authority to act for God."

Priesthood Session

Priesthood is the power and authority of God dele-
gated to man on earth to act in all things for the salvation of men. Those of us who hold this great power
are expected to use it for the purposes for which
it was given to us—to save souls, to save our own soul,
and to lead our Father's children to eternal life in
his kingdom.

141

Everyone of us who holds the priesthood represents the Lord Jesus Christ; we stand in his place and stead in ministering to our fellowmen. We are expected to do what the Lord would do under the same circumstances. Within the field and sphere of our assignments, we are to do what the Lord wants done. We are to use the priesthood to bless ourselves and to bless mankind.

We all hold the priesthood, but our assignments are to labor in various callings in the priesthood. Those who hold the Aaronic Priesthood are expected to do the work that goes with the calling they hold. This lesser priesthood is also designed to prepare men to receive the greater priesthood. And when we receive the Melchizedek Priesthood, we covenant to magnify our calling in it, and the Lord promises to give us eternal life in his kingdom.

Now, my counsel and my plea to all those who hold the priesthood is that they magnify their callings. To do this, we must learn what is expected of us and then do it. We must live by every word that proceedeth forth from the mouth of God. We must keep the commandments and serve our fellowmen to the best of our ability.

This is the Lord's work. We hold his priesthood. He has given it to us by the opening of the heavens in this day. There is no power or authority like it in all this world. It is the power of God.

Members of the First Presidency confer on matters, not only in the office but also when they are out on assignment.

President Joseph Fielding Smith delivered five addresses during the first all-British area general conference.

40

"Every person who receives the light of the gospel becomes a light and a guide to all those whose lives he touches."

A Light Breaking Forth

Tearful eyes watched and voices were muted as President Joseph Fielding Smith stood at the conclusion of the first all-British general conference. As he stood, the audience came to its feet. No one moved as the Prophet left the rostrum. It was as though they did not want to leave the spirit which had prevailed in the meeting. There was a sacred air about King's Hall, and as a testimony to the presence of the spirit, the audience burst into simultaneous singing of "We Thank Thee, O God, for a Prophet."

The hymn ended, but the crowd lingered, hungry for the sweetness of the occasion. There was quiet for a moment, and then their voices raised in "God Be With You Till We Meet Again." This hymn was sung with quivering voices, as the Saints poured out their feelings.

Again they were quiet, but only for a moment. Applause rang out as a last expression of appreciation for the conference and the spirit it brought.

Closing Session

We now come to the close of a wonderful and memorable conference—a general conference of the Church held on British soil, and I hope this becomes a pattern for what shall be in other nations and places.

I feel that the Church will prosper in Great Britain to a far greater degree than has been the case in the past. In the days of Brigham Young and Heber C. Kimball and Wilford Woodruff, and the other apostles and missionaries sent here by the voice of the Spirit, a rich harvest of souls was brought into the kingdom. These choice people gathered with the Saints in America and became a great source of strength and leadership.

Today, however, we have moved into a new era of Church growth and expansion. We are now taking the gospel to the ends of the earth and seeking to build up the kingdom in every nation and among every people, as rapidly as we have the strength to do so.

Several stakes of Zion, a temple dedicated to the Lord, a considerable number of ward and stake buildings, and some highly successful missionary work, all testify to the fact that the Church is coming of age in Great Britain and being built up and strengthened here among some of the best people on earth.

We expect to see this growth continue until the gospel becomes a leavening, sanctifying influence throughout this whole land. The gospel is for all men, and the Church shall be established everywhere, in all nations, even to the ends of the earth, before the second coming of the Son of Man.

It is your responsibility to build up the kingdom here among your own people. The Latter-day Saints, wherever they may be, are and should be a light to the world. The gospel is a light breaking forth in darkness, and every person who receives the light of the gospel becomes a light and a guide to all those whose lives he touches.

Your responsibility here in Great Britain is to be living witnesses of the truth and divinity of the work.

We hope you will live the gospel and work out your own salvation, and that others seeing your good works may be led to glorify our Father in heaven.

Now, once more before we close this conference, I testify that the work in which we are engaged is true. It is the Lord's work and it shall not fail. He has set his hand the second time to gather Israel into the Church, and this time he will raise up congregations of his saints in all nations. His work cannot be stopped. You have had and will have difficulties to overcome, obstacles to surmount, but the Lord's work shall triumph and his purpose shall prevail. Truth always prevails in the end, and this work is true.

President Smith has given a lifetime of service to the Church.

41

His life has been a
continual expression of service
and devotion to
his family, his fellowmen,
and the Church.

A Devoted Prophet

President Joseph Fielding Smith is a man of devotion. His life has been a continual expression of service and devotion to his family, his fellowmen, and the Church.

As a young man he responded to the call of his midwife mother to hook up the horse and drive her on a house call. For hours he sat in the buggy, and though he wondered why it seemed that all babies were born in the middle of the night, he performed a great service for his mother and the mothers of the community.

He has always been devoted to the principles of the gospel. As a teenage boy he broke his leg while paying his tithing.

"We were doing our own farming. With my brother Ira, we had loaded the last load of hay. It was the tithing load, and it was stacked high. We really had about two loads on one hayrack.

"My brother was driving. He was on the front, and I was on the back. The binding poles were sloping up toward the back and securely fastened as we drove to the tithing office," President Smith recalls.

149

From the top of the stack there was a good view of Salt Lake City, and the ride from the field to town had been a pleasant and interesting one. Both boys nestled in the fresh hay and relaxed for the ride.

"When we got to the tithing office," President Smith says, "we had to go through a gate. It had a bar across the top. I wasn't paying any attention to that bar and it swept me off. I went down, kerplunk, right on the ground. The fall broke my leg."

Later when asked "Did the experience strengthen your testimony of tithing?" President Smith replied, "It gave me a testimony that I don't like to have broken legs."

This was not his only experience of devotion involving a broken bone. He slipped on the steps of his apartment one morning on his way to a meeting in the Salt Lake Temple.

"I felt that I had to be at my meeting, so I continued to walk down South Temple Street. Every step I took was painful," he said. He attended the meeting and then walked back to his apartment, still in pain.

"I thought I had sprained my ankle, but when it kept hurting I went to the doctor. He took an X ray of my leg and there were three broken bones, and I had been walking on it," he said.

His devotion to his fellowmen, whether providing a winter coat for a missionary who was without or walking the floor with a sick child, was always warm and complete.

"Dad would always look out for the one in the family who was sick so Mother could care for the rest of the family," his daughter, Mrs. Bruce R. McConkie, recalls. "It was almost fun to be sick because I knew Dad would tend me. He used to get big, beautiful oranges, peel them, and feed them to me a section at a time. He would bring in his old Edison phonograph and play good music. If a march were playing, he would march around the room; if beautiful music were playing, he would dance around to entertain us."

"Don't turn those away who are in need," President Smith taught his family.

"Once a little lady came peddling goods at our house," Mrs. McConkie recalls. "I looked at what she had to sell but could see nothing I wanted, so I sent her away. Dad called to me and asked if I had helped the lady, and I had to tell him no."

"I don't like to see you turn away those who are in need," he said. Giving some money to his daughter, he sent her to find the woman. "I looked all over for that woman, and learned a good lesson that day," Mrs. McConkie said.

President and Sister Smith greeted spectators during Days of '47 Children's Parade in Salt Lake City in July, 1970.

APPENDIX I

A TIME OF PREPARATION
Activities and Travels
of Joseph Fielding Smith
Before Becoming President

1876—Born on July 19 in Salt Lake City to Julina
Lambson Smith and Joseph F. Smith, sixth
President of the Church and son of Hyrum
Smith, brother of the Prophet Joseph Smith.

1896—Married Louie Emyla Shurtliff in April. (She
died in March, 1908, leaving two daughters.)

1896—Received patriarchal blessing from Patriarch
to the Church John Smith. Blessing said, "It is
thy privilege to live to a good old age and the
will of the Lord that you should become a
mighty man in Israel . . . thou shalt realize . . .
that thy life has been preserved for a wise
purpose . . . thou has much to do in order to
complete thy mission upon the earth. It shall
be thy duty to sit in counsel with thy brethren
and to preside among the people."

1897—Ordained an elder.

1899—Entered the British Mission as a seventy.

1901—Began nine-year service as a home missionary in
Salt Lake Stake.

1901—Employed October 4 as a clerk in Church Historian's Office.

1903—Set apart as president of the 24th Quorum of
Seventy.

1903—Became a member of the YMMIA general board;
served until 1919.

1904—Made a librarian in Church Historian's Office
January 1.

1904—Appointed a member of high council of Salt Lake Stake.

1906—Sustained at general conference in April as an assistant Church historian; served until 1921.

1908—Married Ethel Georgina Reynolds; they had five sons and four daughters. (She died in 1937.)

1910—Sustained a member of the Council of the Twelve April 7. Ordained an apostle at age 33 by his father, Joseph F. Smith.

1912—Became a member of the board of trustees of Brigham Young University.

1915—Made a counselor in the presidency of Salt Lake Temple. Served as counselor under two presidents, Anthon H. Lund and George F. Richards, until 1935.

1917—Appointed to Church Board of Education.

1921—Named March 17 to be Church Historian, a position he held until 1970.

1922—Named secretary and director of Genealogical Society.

1927—Became a member of the Deseret Sunday School general board; served until 1935.

1934—Named president of Genealogical Society; served until 1964.

1938—Married on April 12 to Jessie Evans, operatic contralto and long-time member of the Tabernacle Choir. (She died August 3, 1971.)

1939—Filled special assignment in Europe, visiting England, Holland, Belgium, France, Switzerland, Sweden, Norway, Denmark, and Germany. He was in Germany when World War II broke out and, at the request of the First Presidency, directed the evacuation of all American missionaries from Europe. The tour lasted from May until November.

1945—Became president of Salt Lake Temple on June 8. At this time he held the following positions simultaneously: member of Council of the Twelve, president of Genealogical Society, Church Historian, chairman of the General Church Melchizedek Priesthood Committee, member of the Church Board of Education, and chairman of the Church committee on publications.

1950—Became Acting President of the Council of the Twelve following the death of President George F. Richards on August 8.

1951—Made President of the Council of the Twelve on April 9 when David O. McKay became ninth President of the Church.

1951—Awarded honorary Doctor of Letters degree June 4 from BYU for "spiritual scholarship."

1953—Awarded Honorary Master M-Man pin by YMMIA.

1955—Toured Far East for three months and dedicated four countries for the preaching of the gospel.

1956—Cited for being "outstanding player of the Church" at the All-Church softball tournament.

1958—Made three-week tour of England for the dedication of the temple there and visited Switzerland. Later the same year the Smiths toured New Zealand and Australia.

1960—Toured South and Central American missions, noting that the members' spirit "is excellent."

1960—Received Special Service Award at BYU commencement June 3.

1962—Annual Days of '47 pioneer pageant, *Valiantly Onward,* dedicated in July to him.

1962—Presented brigadier general's uniform, red jacket and gray pants, during graduation ceremonies for youths attending Freedom Academy at Camp Williams (Utah) in August.

1963—Completed one-month visit to Australia, his second trip there in five years.

1964—Received Minuteman award from Utah National Guard.
1965—Called on October 29, along with Elder Thorpe B. Isaacson, to be a counselor to President David O. McKay in the First Presidency.
1965—Honored by Beneficial Life Insurance Company in December for more than 50 years of service with the company.
1966—Honored to have BYU collection of historical books named after him.
1967—Presented in February with life-size bronze bust created by Dr. Avard Fairbanks, a gift of the Ensign Stake M-Men and Gleaners.

Many dignitaries from many walks of life meet with President Smith in the Church Office Building. General William C. Westmoreland, U.S. Army chief of staff, accompanied by Elder Marion D. Hanks, Assistant to the Twelve, and Major General Maurice L. Watts, Utah adjutant general, talks with the President in February, 1970.

APPENDIX II

A Time of Fulfillment

Activities and Travels
of Joseph Fielding Smith
Since Becoming President

1970

January 23—Ordained and set apart by the Council of Twelve as the tenth President of The Church of Jesus Christ of Latter-day Saints. President Harold B. Lee, President of the Council and first counselor to President Smith, was voice in the ordination.

January 24—Held his first press conference with his counselors in the Church Office Building.

February 19—Hosted General William C. Westmoreland, U.S. Army Chief of Staff and former commanding general of U.S. forces in Vietnam.

March 8—Traveled to Los Angeles, California, to reorganize presidency of Los Angeles Temple. Set apart Myrthus W. Evans as president.

April 4—Presided over the first general conference of the Church since becoming President.

April 6—Was sustained as President of the Church in solemn assembly in the Salt Lake Tabernacle on Temple Square.

May 1—Awarded an honorary life membership in the Sons of Utah Pioneers, the third consecutive Church President to be so honored.

May 2—Addressed some 200 handicapped seminary students from throughout the western United States.

May 3—Honored by 8,000 University of Utah students at their annual spring fireside in the Tabernacle.

May 4—Received a bound volume with 2,000 signatures of Utah State University students, representing an expression "by written word of our support of the Church and its programs, and in particular, of our support of you as our leader."

May 15—Hosted Swiss Ambassador to the United States, Felix Schnyder, who was visiting in Salt Lake City.

May 21—Hosted 44 Church members from Monte Corona Branch in Mexico, who had traveled to Salt Lake City on a trip to the Mesa Temple.

May 22—Hosted Afioga Afoafouvale Misimoa from Samoa, secretary-general of the South Pacific Commission, which is to the South Pacific what the United Nations is to the world.

June 6—Named with his counselors as editors of the three new Church magazines, the *Ensign*, the *New Era*, and the *Friend*.

June 10—Participated in a banquet, climaxing the month-long "Operation Good Samaritan," which was designed to help a Negro congregation in Salt Lake City raise funds for construction of its chapel.

June 28—Addressed an estimated 7,000 stake and ward MIA leaders in June Conference session in the Tabernacle.

July 12—Spoke to more than 5,000 Mexican Saints in conference sessions in two different stakes in Mexico City. Addresses climaxed week-long trip to Mexico, his first outside United States since becoming President.

July 19—Commemorated 94th birthday anniversary.

July 24—Was grand marshal for the annual Days of '47 parade in Salt Lake City.

July 24—Hosted President Richard M. Nixon in the Church Office Building during visit by the Chief Executive to Salt Lake City.

August 31—Traveled to Mesa, Arizona, for reorganization of presidency of Arizona Temple. Set apart
C. Bryant Whiting as president.

September 7—Presided at cornerstone laying ceremony
of the Ogden (Utah) Temple.

September 11-19—Traveled to Hawaii for whirlwind
visit of the Saints in Hawaii; gave two addresses, including one commemorating fifteenth
anniversary of founding of Church College of
Hawaii; met with missionaries at Language
Training Mission and in Honolulu, and was honored at receptions, banquets and dinners.

September 25—Published his twenty-fifth book, *Seek
Ye Earnestly.*

October 2-4—Presided at 140th Semiannual General
Conference of the Church in the Tabernacle.

October 9—Hosted noted composer, Countess Delores
Mertens of Hamburg, Germany, who had dedicated two songs to the Tabernacle Choir.

October 11—Honored by 3,000 Weber State College
students and townspeople at President's Honor
Night in Ogden, Utah.

October 18—Addressed 800 missionaries at Language
Training Mission at Brigham Young University.

October 20—Reorganized the Idaho Falls Temple
presidency. Set apart Cecil E. Hart as president.

October 31—Met with President Richard M. Nixon for
second time in three months. President Nixon
gave political speech in Tabernacle.

November 8—Reorganized St. George Temple presidency. Set apart Reed Whipple as president.

November 9—Spoke to 400 seminary and institute
students in St. George area.

November 11—Spoke at funeral services for Elder
Thorpe B. Isaacson, Assistant to the Twelve
and former member of the First Presidency.

November 18—Spoke at funeral services for Mrs.

Emma Ray Riggs McKay, widow of the late
President David O. McKay.
November 20—Hosted Argentina Ambassador to the
United States, Pedro Eduardo Real, during
his two-day visit to Utah.
December 19—Issued Christmas message of peace and
goodwill to members of the Church through-
out the world.

1971

January 10—Spoke to nearly 10,000 persons at Utah
State University Assembly Center.
January 12—Received the Archibald F. Bennett Ge-
nealogical Award at Brigham Young University,
given annually by the BYU Society for Local
History and Genealogy to the person who has
done the most to further the principles of
genealogy.
February 7—Honored by University First Stake in
Salt Lake City; received plaque for "Gospel
Scholarship."
March 7—Addressed Wells Stake conference in Salt
Lake City.
March 21—Addressed Riverside Stake conference in
Salt Lake City.
April 2—Addressed thousands of Primary workers
gathered in the Tabernacle for annual Primary
conference.
April 3-4, 6—Presided at sessions of the 141st Annual
General Conference of the Church in the Taber-
nacle.
April 12—Observed with wife, Jessie Evans Smith,
their thirty-third wedding anniversary.
April 18—Addressed 13,000 young people from 46
southern California stakes in Long Beach,
California.

April 25—Dedicated the Laguna Hills Ward in El Toro, California.

May 2—Addressed Valley View Stake conference in Salt Lake City.

May 7—Addressed graduates at Ricks College baccalaureate in Rexburg, Idaho.

May 15—Honored at Snow Day at Snow College in Ephraim, Utah; given plaque expressing "thanks for living a life worthy of receiving the Lord's revelations to the children of the world."

May 21—Presided at cornerstone-laying ceremonies for the Provo Temple.

May 28—Spoke to students of Southern Utah State College in Cedar City.

May 31—Traveled to Independence, Missouri, for dedication of new visitors center, located on portion of original temple site.

June 8—Spoke at the fiftieth anniversary of education weeks at Brigham Young University.

June 20—Addressed Grant Stake conference in Salt Lake City.

June 22—Addressed 29 mission presidents at 1971 mission presidents' seminar.

June 27—Addressed stake and mission MIA leaders at June Conference in the Tabernacle.

July 19—Observed 95th birthday anniversary.

July 24—Was grand marshal at Days of '47 parade.

August 5—Attended funeral services for his wife, Jessie Evans Smith, in the Salt Lake Tabernacle.

August 27-29—Presided over first area general conference of the Church in Manchester, England; gave five speeches, stressing role of British Saints and the worldwide aspect of the Church.

President Smith annually gets together with his family for his birthday observance in Salt Lake City.

APPENDIX III

Spanning the History
of the Church

During the 60 years that Joseph Fielding Smith was a member of the Council of Twelve, before being named President of the Church on January 23, 1970, he served with 42 apostles—men whose lives span nearly the entire history of the Church.

He was called to the Council on April 7, 1910, by his father, Joseph F. Smith, sixth President of the Church, who was born November 13, 1838, in Far West, Missouri, only eight years after the Church had been organized.

When President Smith was called to the Council, the First Presidency consisted of his father, who was ordained an apostle in 1866, as President; Anthon H. Lund, named an apostle in 1889, first counselor; and John Henry Smith, called as an apostle in 1880, second counselor.

The Council of Twelve included Francis M. Lyman, President, ordained in 1880; Heber J. Grant, 1882; Rudger Clawson, 1898; Reed Smoot, 1900; Hyrum Mack Smith, 1901; George Albert Smith, 1903; Charles W. Penrose, 1904; George F. Richards, 1906; Orson F. Whitney, 1906; David O. McKay, 1906; Anthony W. Ivins, 1907; and Joseph Fielding Smith, 1910.

During the next 60 years, 28 apostles were called as members of the Twelve. They were James E. Talmage, 1911; Stephen L Richards, 1917; Richard R. Lyman, 1918; Melvin J. Ballard, 1919; John A. Widtsoe, 1921; Joseph F. Merrill, 1931; Charles A. Callis, 1933; J. Reuben Clark, Jr., 1934; Alonzo A. Hinckley, 1934; Albert E. Bowen, 1937; Sylvester Q. Cannon, 1938; Harold B. Lee, 1941; Spencer W. Kimball, 1943; Ezra Taft Benson, 1943; Mark E. Petersen, 1944; Matthew

Cowley, 1945; Henry D. Moyle, 1947; Delbert L. Stapley, 1950; Marion G. Romney, 1951; LeGrand Richards, 1952; Adam S. Bennion, 1953; Richard L. Evans, 1953; George Q. Morris, 1954; Hugh B. Brown, 1958; Howard W. Hunter, 1959; Gordon B. Hinckley, 1961; N. Eldon Tanner, 1962; and Thomas S. Monson, 1963.

Since becoming President, President Smith has called one apostle to the Council: Boyd K. Packer, named in 1970.

President Smith has also worked with four Patriarchs to the Church, 22 members of the First Council of Seventy, five Presiding Bishops, and 27 Assistants to the Twelve.

APPENDIX IV

Books Written by President Joseph Fielding Smith

1. —1901—Asael Smith of Topsfield
2. —1905—Blood Atonement and the Origin of Plural Marriage
3. —1909—Origin of the Reorganized Church and the Question of Succession
4. —1922—Essentials in Church History
5. —1928—Seeking After Our Dead
6. —1931—The Way to Perfection
7. —1936—The Progress of Man
8. —1938—The Life of Joseph F. Smith
9. —1938—Teachings of the Prophet Joseph Smith
10. —1942—Signs of the Times
11. —1944—The Restoration of All Things
12. —1953—Church History and Modern Revelation, Volume I
13. —1953—Church History and Modern Revelation, Volume II
14. —1954—Man: His Origin and Destiny
15. —1954—Doctrines of Salvation, Volume I
16. —1955—Doctrines of Salvation, Volume II
17. —1956—Doctrines of Salvation, Volume III
18. —1957—Answers to Gospel Questions, Volume I
19. —1957—Elijah the Prophet and His Mission and Salvation Universal
20. —1958—Answers to Gospel Questions, Volume II
21. —1960—Answers to Gospel Questions, Volume III
22. —1963—Answers to Gospel Questions, Volume IV
23. —1966—Answers to Gospel Questions, Volume V
24. —1966—Take Heed to Yourselves
25. —1970—Seek Ye Earnestly

INDEX

167